Glassbead Books

JOHN HOLBO, EDITOR

Looking For a Fight

Is There a Republican
War on Science?

Edited by John Holbo

a CROOKED TIMBER book event

Parlor Press
West Lafayette, Indiana
www.parlorpress.com

Parlor Press LLC, West Lafayette, Indiana 47906
Printed in the United States of America
© 2006 by Parlor Press.

S A N: 2 5 4 - 8 8 7 9

Library of Congress Cataloging-in-Publication Data
Looking for a fight : is there a Republican war on science? / edited by John Holbo.
   p. cm. -- (Glassbead books)
  "A Crooked timber book event."
  ISBN 1-932559-91-4 (pbk. : alk. paper) -- ISBN 1-932559-92-2 (adobe ebook)
  1. Science and state--United States. 2. Republicanism--United States. I. Holbo, John, 1967-
  Q127.U6L66 2006
  509.7309'051--dc22
                2006028922

The book you are holding—*if* you are holding a book—is available as a free PDF download. Visit HTTP://WWW.PARLORPRESS.COM

This book was designed and edited by John Holbo. Text is set in 11 point Adobe Garamond Pro. and printed on acid-free paper.

Parlor Press, LLC is an independent publisher of scholarly and trade titles in print and multimedia formats. This book is available in paper and Adobe eBook formats from Parlor Press on the World Wide Web at http://www.parlorpress.com or through online and brick-and-mortar bookstores. For submission information or to find out about Parlor Press publications, write to Parlor Press, 816 Robinson St., West Lafayette, Indiana, 47906, or email editor@parlorpress.com.

Chris Mooney's *The Republican War On Science* is published by
Basic Books (hardback, 2005; paperback 2006). Visit the **book
site** for excerpts, reviews, author information, updates, etc.

http://www.waronscience.com/home.php

This 'book event' consisted of a series of posts about Mooney's
book on Crooked Timber (crookedtimber.org). The event
was organized by John Quiggin. Readers met author, semi-
nar-style; still more readers left comments, blog-style. For this
book, the posts have been edited for typos, clarity, style and
suitability for a slightly different medium. Page numbers for
Mooney's book have been updated to match the paperback
version. A few substantial edits have been made at authors'
discretion. To view the unedited original posts and comments
click the links at the end of each entry. The event archive as a
whole has a permanent URL:

http://crookedtimber.org/category/chris-mooney-seminar/

Paper has been a bit of a puzzle. We have opted to make it
typographically clear where links appear in the electronic version. Readers of the paper version who wish to follow links
can download the PDF version of the book from Parlor Press,
or check the original posts.

contents

Looking For a Fight

① Republican War on Science: Introduction to a Seminar

JOHN QUIGGIN ▶

Political conflict over scientific issues has probably never been as sharp as at present. Issues like global warming and stem-cell research that came to prominence in the 1990s are being fiercely debated. At the same time, questions that had, apparently, been resolved long ago, like evolution or the US ban on agricultural use of DDT, are being refought. A striking feature of these debates is that, in nearly all cases (the one big exception being GM foods) the fight lines up the political Right, and particularly the US Republican Party, on one side, and the majority of scientists and scientific organisations on the other. Chris Mooney's book, *The Republican War on Science*, is, therefore, a timely contribution to the debate, and we are happy to host a seminar to discuss it, and thank Chris for agreeing to take part.

In addition to contributions from five members of CT, we're very pleased to have two guests participating in the debate. Tim Lambert has been an active participant in the blogospheric version of some of the debates discussed by Chris. Tim, like the CT participants, broadly endorses Chris' argument, though with some disagreement on analytical points and questions of emphasis and presentation. To broaden the debate, Steve Fuller was invited to take part in the seminar, and kindly agreed, knowing that he would be very much in the minority. Steve presents a social constructivist critique of Chris' argument. We're very grateful to Steve for taking part.

I won't attempt to summarise the debate since Chris Mooney, in his response, has done an excellent job.

originally posted on March 27th, 2006
http://crookedtimber.org/2006/03/27/republican-war-on-science-intro-duction-to-a-seminar/

② The Republican War on Science

HENRY FARRELL ▶

Books about the politics of science policy and other complicated policy areas have a hard time doing justice to the politics
and the technical aspects both; they usually emphasize one
and underplay the other. On the one hand, many journalistic
accounts ham up the politics and underplay the analysis, doc-
umenting the atrocities, one after another after another. Raw
outrage supported by anecdotes gets partisans' juices flowing,
but it's not likely to persuade the unpersuaded, or provide any
good understanding of how to solve the problem (other than
to kick the bums out, which is a start, but only a start.) On
the other, there are books that do an excellent job of discussing the underlying policy issues, but that lack political zing.
Marion Nestle's *Food Politics* is a good example; it provides a
nuanced (and utterly damning) account of how the technical
processes of food regulation have been corrupted by special
interests, but it's written by a policy wonk for policy wonks.
There's lots and lots of technical nitty gritty. The good news
is that Chris Mooney's book pulls off the difficult double act
of talking about the politics in a fresh and immediate fashion while paying attention to the underlying issues of institutions and policies, and does it with considerable aplomb. *The
Republican War on Science* is written with an eye for a good
story, but it still has a real intellectual punch. There's an un-

derlying argument as to why the relationship between science and politics is in a parlous state. While I think that there's an interesting piece missing from this argument (on which more below), it links the very different issues of science politics under the current administration (regulation, intelligent design, global warming, stem cell research) into a more-or-less coherent narrative.

One of the key moments in Mooney's story—the tragedy of modern science policy—was the decision of the Gingrich Congress to get rid of Congress's Office of Technology Assessment (OTA), which provided impartial assessments of scientific issues that had policy implications in the 1990s. As Mooney documents, there were a number of reasons for this. The Congress claimed to want to cut down on 'government waste'; getting rid of OTA was a cheap way to demonstrate their commitment to doing this. OTA was sometimes slow to deliver its reports (although it was widely lauded for doing an excellent job.) But the key problem, in the eyes of Gingrich Republicans, was that its reports were often politically inconvenient. OTA had made a number of enemies during the Reagan era, by issuing reports which reflected the scientific consensus on the "Star Wars" program of missile defence—that it was unworkable, and stood a significant chance of "catastrophic failure". That these claims were true did little to endear them to Star Wars' defenders. The result was that some Republicans began to see OTA as an enemy stronghold. Mooney's account makes it clear that this wasn't an universal perception among Republicans—one moderate Republican congressman mounted a defence of OTA that might well have succeeded. Unfortunately, this last-ditch initiative failed.

Of course, the demise of OTA isn't the only factor contributing to the corruption of science politics. However, it did play a quite significant role. OTA was the most important structure through which impartial science advice could enter the policy-making process, and commercial interests and religious fundamentalists have rushed to fill the vacuum that it left. While there were abuses of science under the Reagan administration, and indeed under previous Democratic administrations too, they weren't systemic. As Mooney argues, they are now. To mention only some of the corruptions of the policy process that he discusses at length, the "Data Quality Act," an Orwellian misnomer if ever there was one, tries to give business an effective veto power over scientific advice. Tobacco firms pioneered political attacks on "junk science" (i.e. science that suggested that smoking was bad for your health) and sought to magnify scientific uncertainty, writing a playbook that oil companies and others eagerly adopted. (In the words of a Brown and Williamson internal document, "doubt is our product.") Senators like James Inhofe blatantly misrepresented and continue to misrepresent the scientific consensus on climate change so that they could claim that man-made global warming was a "hoax … perpetrated on the American people." Bogus "sound science" arguments are used to attack the Endangered Species Act. George W. Bush makes patently incorrect claims about stem cell research in order to block federal funding. And so on.

A second, even more troubling set of attacks go hand-in-hand with the corruption of the policy making process, amounting to an attack on the basic norms of the scientific community—peer review, principled argument, and the reaching of (always tentative, always open to revision, but nonetheless real) consensus on issues where the science on a topic appears to be more or less settled. The "intelligent design" movement is a quite deliberate and conscious attempt to drive a wedge into this consensus (or the public perception of this consensus), to make it appear that there is substantive scientific debate where there is none. So too, global warming contrarians, and, a couple decades ago, people who denied the link between CFCs and ozone depletion. Websites like Steven Milloy's JUNKSCIENCE.COM exist in order to spread doubt, and to make non-debates appear to be real controversies.

Mooney's book delivers a damning indictment precisely because it shows that these various abuses aren't unrelated; they're all symptoms of the same problem, a deep-seated corruption of the policy process, linked to an attack on the basic principles of scientific integrity. Disinterested scientific advice is increasingly marginalized both in policy and in public debate. Just last week, a *New York Times* journalist gave near-equal hearing to biologists and Intelligent Design cranks, defending this with the claim that it's the controversy that is newsworthy. The problem is deep-rooted; Mooney argues that the solution isn't simply to turf Republicans out of office. Indeed, he claims that "[e]ncouraging the electoral success of Republican moderates with good credentials on science could potentially have just as constructive an effect as backing Democrats." More fundamental institutional reforms are needed, both to the policy process and to the ways in which journalists and others report public debates on scientific issues.

This is a terrific book—I strongly recommend it. There is however, one piece of the puzzle that's missing: Mooney does an excellent job of describing the consequences of the Republican relationship with science, but misses out on some of its causes and intellectual justifications. There's a complex ideological knot there that needs to be unentangled. The 'anti-science' agenda of the modern right wing often goes hand-in-hand with an infatuation with the power of technology. Newt Gingrich is the prime example (Mooney more or less admits that there's something he doesn't get about Gingrich)—on the one hand presiding over the gutting of the infrastructure of science policy advice, but on the other pushing for a major increase in NSF funding. What gives? I think there's an ideological substrate to a certain flavour of Republicanism, which finds its purest form in a certain kind of science fiction (the "competent man" SF of the 1940's and 1950's) and extropian varieties of libertarianism. Here we encounter the implicit belief that science doesn't impose limits, but instead provides tools, and that there's no problem that can't be solved by a combination of engineering prowess and can-do spirit. This combines a dislike for science, when it suggests, say, that the environment can be seriously degraded by human activity, with a boundless optimism in technology's ability to solve whatever problems we face, and an underlying faith in a universe of effectively limitless resources. Thus the dislike for scientific consensus, whenever it says that we face constraints on our freedom of action, e.g. the faith that Star Wars would work, despite the many good reasons for believing that it wouldn't. Hence also the refusal to believe that global warming is a real problem. This set of beliefs clearly has a strong elective affinity with pro-market values and is doubtless often highly convenient for business interests (hence the continued funding for TECH CENTRAL STATION). But it can't simply be reduced to a cynical smoke screen for material interests—there's a real set of social beliefs there. Indeed, it's a set of beliefs that is sometimes justified in practice—we do often underestimate the ability of human ingenuity to solve problems. However, at the end of the day it's based on faith (in the boundless powers of human creativity) rather than science; there are material limits to our powers, even if we may sometimes be mistaken about where those limits lie. This secular religion—which has far fewer followers than religious fundamentalism but rather more intellectual coherence—helps explain the ideological staying power of the anti-science tendency in the modern Republican movement.

originally posted August 30th, 2005

http://crookedtimber.org/2005/08/30/the-republican-war-on-science/

③ War on Science

TED BARLOW ❭

I had to be on guard while reading Chris Mooney's *The Republican War on Science*, because it's a sterling example of a book that tells me what I want to hear. For the lion's share of the readers of this blog, it's what you want to hear, too. So take this with a grain of salt.

Mooney does not argue that Republicans or conservatives are anti-science in the way of the forces of liberalism are alleged to be anti-Christmas or pro-death. There's no doubt that Republicans enjoy their iPods and CT scanners as much as Democrats.

Rather, he believes that the leadership of the Republican party has taken specific steps to reduce the power of the scientific consensus on public policy. Mooney largely ignores the low-hanging fruit of conservative commentators, who barely appear in the book. Instead, the book predominantly focuses on top policymakers in Congress and the White House. In one thread, Mooney tells the story of how the Gingrich Congress eliminated the Office of Technology Assessment (OTA), a scientific body that used to provide Congress with independent expert analysis of science issues.

> "Gingrich's view was always, 'I'll set up one-on-one interactions between members of Congress and key members of the scientific community,'" recalls Bob Palmer, former Democratic staff

director of the House Committee on Science. "Which I thought was completely bizarre. I mean, who comes up with these people, and who decides they're experts, and what member of Congress really wants to do that?"

It wasn't long before this latitude was abused. Rep. Senator James Inhofe, the man who called the EPA a "gestapo bureaucracy" and who famously suggested that manmade global warming was "the greatest hoax ever perpetrated on the American people", was awarded the chairmanship of the Senate Environment and Public Works Committee in 1999. Mooney relates how Inhofe reacted to the solidifying scientific consensus on global warming. Says Mooney, "The IPCC, the National Academy of Sciences, the American Meteorological Society, the American Geophysical Union—all agree that human activity is causing climate change" (p. 84).

Inhofe led a committee hearing in 2003 which set two global warming sceptics with ties to the energy industry against one scientist, Michael Mann, to represent the mainstream view. Mooney again:

> At Inhofe's hearing, Mann defended both his own work and the conclusions of the IPCC, which channels the work of hundreds of experts. But for those keeping track of the Senate that day, the intellectual ticker showed a score of two to one, not a handful versus a horde. Such was Inhofe's conception of "balance." At one point, for example, the senator asked the panelists whether they agreed or disagreed that rising carbon dioxide levels can "produce many beneficial effects on the natural plant and animal environments of the earth." Here were the results:

DR. SOON: I agree.

DR. MANN: I find little there to agree with.

DR. LEGATES: I would tend to agree.

> ... By now, the problems with Inhofe's attempt to turn Congress into a science court should be apparent. The validity of Michael Mann's particular "hockey stick" analysis remains open to debate among experts, and has in fact been prominently challenged in the peer-reviewed literature. But holding a heated public hearing between mainstream scientists and contrarians will hardly help determine its merits. "That's why the federal government turns to the National Academy of the Sciences for advice, or the governments of the world turn to the Intergovernmental Panel on Climate Change," explains Princeton University climate expert Michael Oppenheimer." (pp. 88-89)

The book catalogues a series of incidents in recent years in which the Republican leadership battled, ignored or muddied the mainsteam scientific consensus when it conflicts with the policy preferences of either large industrial interests or fundamentalist Christians.

It's hard to argue that the solutions to all such policy problems —the resolutions of all such political arguments—lie at the bottom of a test tube, or in a climate model. The Republican leaders in question could have made arguments for their positions by arguing that moral or economic criteria sometimes trump science. There's no objectively correct answer to the question of when life begins; if one accepts that a fertilized egg is the moral equivalent of an infant, then it's logical to consider stem-cell research the moral equivalent of murder. Many global warming skeptics have argued that the economic costs of Kyoto-like greenhouse gas emissions measures swamp the forseeable benefits. Mooney mentions legislation protecting food and drink companies from obesity-related lawsuits, which 40% of House Democrats voted for, and which many people (including me) would be happy to support, even knowing the connection between fast food and obesity.

What is not acceptable is the distortion of science to win the argument. Mooney argues (successfully, I think) that this has become a common modus operandi when the scientific consensus threatens the policy preferences of a Republican interest group.

originally posted March 27th, 2006
http://crookedtimber.org/2006/03/27/war-on-science/

④ Worldwide War on Science

JOHN QUIGGIN ❭

What do evolution, human-caused global warming and the adverse health effects of exposure to cigarette smoking have in common? All are well-established scientific facts and all have been vigorously denied by a network of think-tanks, politicians and commentators associated with the Republican Party in the United States.

Of course, disputes over environmental and health issues have been going on for many years, and evolution has always been controversial in the United States. The striking development of the last fifteen years or so is the development of a systematic approach hostile to, and subversive of, all the standard rules of scientific inquiry and treatment of evidence. This approach is referred to by Chris Mooney as *The Republican War on Science*.

The central rhetorical element of the War on Science is the abandonment of science, as the term is normally understood, in favour of what is called 'sound science', a term that first came to prominence with The Advancement of Sound Science Coalition, a body primarily funded by the Philip Morris tobacco company. Broadly speaking, 'sound science' is science produced at the behest of relevant industry groups, though mainstream scientific research may be included if its results are politically convenient.

Conversely, 'junk science' is any scientific research that produces results inconsistent with the financial and ideological interests associated with the Republican Party. Not surprisingly, research on the dangers of second-hand smoke has been a prominent target, along with climate science and other environmental research. The 'junk science' approach is most prominently represented at junkscience.com, a site operated by former TASSC head Steven Milloy and hosted by the Cato Institute, one of the network of industry-funded think-tanks that help to promote the attack on science.

Mooney documents the rise of the think-tank network, and the roles of commentators like Rush Limbaugh, industry-funded scientists like Willie Soon and David Legates, and politicians like James Inhofe and Tom DeLay. He presents a series of case studies, covering issues including global warming, stem-cell research, the preservation of endangered species and the effect of dietary sugar intake on obesity. In all these cases, factual conclusions based on extensive scientific research have been challenged, and in many cases rejected, on the basis of purely political considerations.

Even more notable is the way in which the war on science has exploited social norms of discussion to create a situation where proven falsehoods can be treated as defensible positions in public debate, then used as the basis of policy formulation. Particularly in the United States, journalists are inculcated with notions of 'balance' associated with the adage that 'there are two sides to every story'. As a result, any proposition that is supported by a substantial body of opinion is automatically treated as being on a par with any other, even when there is an overwhelming body of scientific evidence on the other side.

Similarly, concepts of peer review and accountability have been used to give business groups opportunities to challenge, and frequently suppress, research that produces conclusions antithetical to their interests. Fine-sounding names like the Data Quality Act are used to disguise political censorship of research.

Creationists have made particularly effective use of norms of fairness to argue that 'Intelligent Design' theory should be taught as an alternative to evolution. Mooney notes the 'Wedge document' prepared by the Discovery Institute in Seattle, which clearly sets out the way in which the nominally non-religious Intelligent Design model can be used as a stalking horse for the reintroduction of Biblical creationism.

Mooney shows how the same strategies, and in many cases the same actors reappear in debates over many different issues, replacing objective scientific analysis with the kind of politicized treatment of evidence familiar from claims about weapons of mass destruction in the leadup to the Iraq war. The Marshall Institute, for example, first appears backing Star Wars, then denying the effects of CFCs on the ozone layer, and finally distorting historical climate records on climate in an effect to discredit research on global warming.

Repeated across almost every field of scientific research, the ultimate effect of the Republican strategy is to constitute a complete parallel universe, in which scientific 'knowledge' is derived from think-tanks and unqualified opinion writers rather than from actual scientists working on the topic in question. Rather than being confronted with actual evidence, approved views are amplified by the echo chamber of repeated mutual quotation until they appear as established facts.

A particularly striking case, discussed relatively briefly by Mooney, is that of DDT. This cheap and persistent insecticide was freely used for all sorts of purposes in the decades after World War II, but its environmental dangers were pointed out by Rachel Carson in her 1962 classic, *Silent Spring*. Carson's book was met with vigorous criticism, but her main claims stood up well to official scrutiny and the US banned the use of DDT in 1972. Although some sniping continued, the case against widescale use of DDT was almost universally accepted.

Since about 2000 however, a pro-DDT campaign has gone into overdrive with the publication of a string of newspaper opinion pieces and other articles, in publications rang-ing from *FoxNews* to the *New York Times*. The central tenet of these pieces is the claim that Carson's book and the resulting US ban on DDT have led to the loss of millions of lives from malaria in developing countries.

It takes only a few minutes work with Google to deter-mine that this story is false in almost every particular. The new stories apparently arose from debates leading up to the 2000 Johannesburg conference on persistent organochlorine pollution, during which some environmental groups advocat-ing setting a date for a phaseout of DDT use. This propos-al was ultimately withdrawn, but the debate produced some overheated pro-DDT rhetoric which was then amplified by the echo-chamber of rightwing think-tanks, and blogs com-mentators into a legend that bears almost no relationship to reality.

There has never been a global ban on DDT use as an an-timalarial, and it has been in continuous use in a number of countries. The abandonment of DDT in particular countries has been mainly due to the development of resistance by mos-quitoes, which has rendered infeasible the original goal of eradication.

The most important remaining use of DDT is as a spray inside houses or huts. This strategy is supported by the agen-cies such as WHO and USAID in some cases, but is common-ly regarded as less effective than the use of insecticide-treated bednets. In middle-income and richer countries, and where resistance is a problem, insecticides other than DDT have been used.

A striking feature of the true story is that bans on the agri-cultural use of DDT (such as the US ban in 1972) have actu-ally saved lives by inhibiting the development of resistance.

The same parallel universe may be observed in relation to global warming. The consensus view, that the increase in greenhouse gases arising from human activity has driven a warming trend that will accelerate in future is backed up by thousands of scientific studies, painstakingly assembled by the IPCC. Against this, Republicans and their allies solemnly quote the work of such luminaries as science fiction writer Michael Crichton and retired mining executive Steven McIntyre.

All of these innovations have been exported to Australia, though they have sometimes struggled to take root here. As in the United States, a large group of commentators has preferred to take its scientific information from the parallel universe created by the Republican machine rather than from mainstream science. Miranda Devine and Michael Duffy have peddled the DDT myth. The Institute of Public Affairs has rejected mainstream science on passive smoking and promoted research commissioned by the (now-dissolved) Tobacco Institute of Australia.

The teaching of creationism is much less of a hot button issue in Australia than in America, partly because belief in Biblical literalism is much weaker here and partly because of public funding of religious schools, which are effectively free to treat the issue as they please. Nevertheless, it has received support in surprising quarters. Right-wing columnist Andrew Bolt, for example, has attacked critics of intelligent design, while maintaining a studied neutraltity regarding his own views on the question. And lobbyists have been pushing the issue to Education Minister Brendan Nelson, who raised the possibility that Intelligent Design might be taught in Australian schools.

The central issue of concern, though, has been global warming. In addition to regular visits from US contrarians, Australia has its own Lavoisier Institute. The adoption of famous names to push positions that would probably have horrified the eponymous individuals is a characteristic feature of the war on science.

Despite valiant attempts, though, the war on science has been far less successful in Australia than in the US. Although the Australian government has fallen into line with the Bush

Administration in opposing the Kyoto protocol, it has repeatedly reaffirmed its support for mainstream climate science.

Not surprisingly, Mooney's book has received plenty of criticism. The first line of argument, made routinely in response to any criticism of the Bush Administration is that their opponents, and in particular Clinton's Democratic Administration, were just as bad. Mooney is prepared for this line and sees it off in his opening pages. While noting some instances of exaggeration or misuse of scientific evidence among opponents of the Republicans, on issues such as genetically modified foods and the short-run therapeutic potential of stem cells, Mooney argues persuasively that these offences are trivial by comparison with the systematic assault on science launched by the Republicans.

One way of defending this conclusion is to compare the range and scale of these spurious claims. It's easy enough to find scientifically dubious claims about the dangers of genetically modified foods, but even these have come mostly from radical green groups, such as Greenpeace, and from individual campaigners. There are few issues on which Democrats in the US, or social democrats and liberals elsewhere, have taken a position that is obviously at variance with the findings of mainstream science. By contrast, there is almost no scientific discipline, from geological analysis of the age of the earth to epidemiology to climate science that has not been subject to ideological attack from Republicans and associated interests.

Even more striking, though, is the institutional record. The Republicans, in Congress and in the Bush Administration, have scrapped or undermined institutions that promoted objective scientific analysis as a basis for policy formation and turned instead to procedures designed to give control to ideologues and financial interest. This process began in the Gingrich era, when the Office of Technology Assessment was scrapped, apparently because of its role in discrediting the Strategic Defensive Initiative missile-defence system, better known as 'Star Wars'. The process has been expanded greatly under Bush

A more subtle and effective criticism, PUT FORWARD BY DANIEL SAREWITZ is that, in effect, the Republicans are right. The kind of purity set forth as an ideal by Mooney, is in Sarewitz's view unattainable.

Mooney's "polemical fervor blinds him to the political content inherent in all discourse that connects science to human affairs."

As an example, Mooney attacks Republicans for making false claims about the usefulness of adult stem cells as a substitute for embryonic stem cells in research. Sarewitz suggests that, since Germany has prohibited embryonic stem cells research, Germans must, by the terms of Mooney's analyis, share a disdain for science with Republicans.

But Sarewitz is missing the point here. Mooney does not deny that it is open to societies to decide, on ethical grounds, to forgo the medical progress that might be achieved as a result of stem cell research. Rather, he suggests that such a decision should be made in the light of the best available evidence on costs and benefits and criticises Republicans for fabricating and distorting that evidence. In his critique, Sarewitz provides no evidence that similar distortion was practised in Germany.

In effect, here we are back to the fact-value distinction that was at the centre of 20th century debates about positivism. In Mooney's view, scientists do their best (or should do their best) to determine the facts that should inform public debate. It is then up to political processes to determine the course of action most consistent with the values held by the public. By contrast, Sarewitz views the two as inextricably entwined, to the point where he does not appear to be aware that such a distinction might be suggested.

In the 20th century, rejection of the fact-value distinction came mostly from the left, first from Marxists who saw all truth-claims made in a class society as being incorrigibly saturated with ideology and then from postmodernists and social constructivists who attacked the whole idea of an independently existing truth, which might be ascertained, or at least approached, by scientific inquiry.

One of the central conceits of postmodernism has been to pluralise abstract nouns like truth, abandoning attempts at a unified view of the world in favour of a celebration of difference. The great lesson learned by postmodern Republicans has been that, where multiple 'truths' contend, the 'truth' favoured by powerful interests is likely to prevail. Since scientific truth is refractory and not amenable to political control, its claims to special privilege must be challenged, in order that politically reliable alternatives such as 'sound science' can replace it.

While the adoption of postmodernist positions has mostly been done without acknowledgement (perhaps because of memories of the 1990s 'Science Wars' when denunciation of postmodernism was *de rigeur* on the right), there have been exceptions. Leading Intelligent Design advocate Philip Johnson has noted the influence of postmodernist critical theory on the development of his views.

The social constructivist position is represented in this seminar by Steve Fuller, who testified on the ID side in the recent Dover court case over the teaching of Intelligent Design, so rather than attempt to summarise it, I'll leave him to put it forward, then respond in discussion.

Mooney suggests a range of institutional responses to these developments most notably the revival of the Office of Technology Assessments. It is clear, however, that the crucial changes involve political debate and its reporting. In particular, it is necessary to overcome the presumption that scientific propositions should be treated as matters of political opinion,

As regards the established media, we have a long way to go. The Australian and US press give more space to ideological attacks on climate science than to the actual findings of science. For example, in the week leading up to the meeting of the Asia-Pacific Climate Pact in Sydney all of the major Australian 'quality' dailies published opinion pieces by contrarians attacking climate science.

The rise of the internet has been a mixed blessing. On the one hand, it has generated an almost hermetically-sealed echo chamber, in which science warriors can circulate, adapt and modify the factoids, talking points and bogus quotations that are the stock in trade of opinion pieces like those mentioned above.

On the other hand, for anyone who is aware of the general strategy adopted by the advocates of 'sound science', resources like Google and Wikipedia provide immediate confirmation in particular instances. In the past, an opinion piece by, say, Steven Milloy, would appear with an uninformative or misleading byline, and would be given the benefit of the doubt by most readers. Now, anyone who performs a basic check can discover, with little effort, the full history of his efforts as tobacco lobbyist and hired gun for polluting industries.

What is needed, therefore is general awareness of the existence of an organised campaign against science, in which the Bush Administration plays a leading role. As Mooney observes, scientists must launch counter-campaigns to blunt the impact of widespread misinformation on the media and public. Merely by making it clear that the war against science is taking place, and that the current leadership of the Republican Party is on the wrong side, scientists will help to change the terms of debate. Winning the debate will require scientists to learn new and unfamiliar ways of communicating, in the face of the professional distortions of the anti-science lobby. Still, even if scientists are sometimes outmanoeuvred in debate, the experience of the debate over intelligent design, the one case where scientists have mounted a concerted response to their intellectual enemies, suggests that truth will out in the end.

originally posted March 27th, 2006
http://crookedtimber.org/2006/03/27/worldwide-war-on-science/

⑤ The Stars and Stripes Down to Earth

DANIEL DAVIES ▌

Chris Mooney's book, *The Republican War on Science*, seems to me a very American book. It's not that Europe is bereft of "sound science" hacks trying to influence the process by which regulations are made, or even of our own brand of home-grown irrationalists of one kind or another. However, America does seem to have a hell of a lot of them, and they seem to pick battlegrounds (like creation science, to take the clearest example) which suggest that the purpose of a lot of the Republican War on Science is not so much to push an alternative pseudo-scientific agenda for political and economic gain, but rather to knock scientists off their pedestal for the sake of doing so.

Because I'm not really familiar with the ins and outs of American regulatory politics which are the meat of TRWOS, I thought I'd pursue this line of thinking a bit further. What I mean to suggest is that to a certain extent Chris has got the causation wrong in his underlying analysis of the Republican War on Science. In other words, it's not so much a case of vested interests wanting to tear down good science in order to replace it with bad science that supports economically convenient conclusions, as a case of the hack science being generated in order to fill a vacuum created by an original desire at the heart of right wing politics to bring down good science for the sake of doing so.

◀ 23

I think that this causal story fits the facts at least as well as the more obvious one and perhaps even a bit better. After all, there is a clear economic interest in trying to ensure that rare species are miscounted or that the impact of pollution is underestimated; there's no need for any other explanation there. But there is rather less obvious economic interest in trying to deny the facts about global warming, still less in pretending that DDT (a commodity chemical) is a panacea for malaria and as far as I can see none at all in "intelligent design". Intelligent design isn't even a particularly congenial theory for fundamentalist Christians to be pushing, as it appears to me to be inconsistent with the literal truth of the Book of Genesis, which was surely the only point in opposing the teaching of evolution in the first place.

So if there's a unifying reason behind all these different phenomena (and it is surely the thesis of TRWOS that there is), then I don't think it can be narrow self-interest. I think it's something more like the "authoritarian irrationalism" that Theodor Adorno identified in books like *The Stars Down To Earth*, and that, in its guise of anti-intellectualism, De Tocqueville identified before that as being particularly common in American public life. I realise that Adorno's theory is right out of fashion these days, but it's always appealed to me and I think it has decent explanatory power over this phenomenon.

There is a particular kind of irrationalism Adorno identified, which is characteristic of authoritarian politics (and therefore also, I hardly need to say, of the kind of authoritarian politics which these days calls itself "libertarian" but never saw a pro-business law it didn't like.) It's rooted in status insecurity and a consequent distrust of ambiguity. Adorno's book carried out an analysis of the astrology columns in the *Los Angeles Times*, demonstrating how their underlying theme was always the same; they encouraged the readers to believe that there was an underlying order to the world, that following simple rules was always the right thing to do, and that behaving in the "right" fashion would always have the right results.

The readers of the astrology column probably didn't believe that the stars controlled their destiny. But, by pretending that they did, they were able to reduce the stress caused by the fact that whatever controlled the readers of the astrology column's lives, they themselves didn't.

This is the root of authoritarian irrationalism. For people who are status-insecure (which Adorno argues is the root of authoritarian politics—he notes that second-generation immigrants systematically score much higher for right-wing politics than other groups), the fact that the real world is a complicated, ambiguous and uncertain place creates intolerable stress. The defensive reaction to this stress is a retreat to somewhere safer and more predictable; a world in which the unpleasant facts of the matter are simply denied and their occasional intrusions explained away as being most likely the result of some shadowy conspiracy.

And when you look at the Republican War on Science through this sort of a lens, it makes a bunch of sense. It is intolerably stressful for technological process to be both good for the economy and bad for the environment. Or for science (which is good) to contradict religion (which is also good). Or for the companies that create the modern world to be also selling us dangerous products. So, the "science" that shows that all of these things are happening has to be denied and rejected. Thus, a world of "sound science" is created, and real science is portrayed as a conspiracy of ideologically motivated men. I think that Mooney is correct to identify "sound science" as a creation of the PR industry, but the PR industry can't create something unless it has some basic desires to work with. If the audience for "sound science" was thinking at all, nobody would be fooled, so we do need a theory of why it is that they aren't thinking, and I think that Adorno's is quite convincing. Or, in other words, it makes no sense for scientists to tear their hair out about the state of science politics and blame it on "the low quality of scientific journalism". There is no other kind of scientific journalism possible. It's certainly not realistic to hope for popular acceptance of confidence intervals, the tentative nature of scientific theories and the differing standards of proof and certainty, because this is just more of the ambiguity that has already been judged intolerable by a large chunk of the American polity in much more diluted form. The underlying problem is one of political psychology and it's not going away.

Which leaves two questions; could there be a "Democratic War on Science", and is this purely an American phenomenon?

I think that the answer to the first is yes there could. There are authoritarians on the political left of the spectrum as well as the right, and I can't help but notice that it is in the American university system that quite sensible French theories of literary criticism have been given a specifically irrationalist interpretation that was never really there in the originals. But I think that the answer to the second is also yes it is. There is a lot of anti-science thinking in Europe (and I'm sure there is in Asia, too, but I don't know much about it.) But it has a much less specifically irrationalist cast to it, using the term in Adorno's sense. It is probably irrational (in the everyday language sense) of Europeans to be so implacably opposed to genetically modified food, but their opposition is not in general cast in "irrationalist" terms; it's based on "despite what the science says, I don't believe it" rather than "the science cannot possibly be saying that because I don't want to believe it." And I don't think that this is a coincidence. Authoritarian politics in general are these days much less common in Europe than in America. I don't know why the politics of status insecurity are more common in the last remaining great world power, or why they have got more rather than less influential since the end of the Cold War, but I suggest that this is the root of the troubled relationship between American politics and American science, and that because of this, the Republican War on Science is likely to get worse rather than better.

originally posted, March 27th, 2006
http://crookedtimber.org/2006/03/27/the-stars-and-stripes-down-to-earth-posted-for-daniel-davies-by-hf/

⑥ Mooney Minus
the Polemic?

JOHN HOLBO ▌

'War on science' sounds halfway between 'war on Christmas' and 'war on terror'; that is, halfway between something that can't possibly be real and something that is real enough, but probably misdescribed. The title hints at a sinister—well, *you* see. The worry is the thing is afflicted with a touch of the paranoid style.

Still, sometimes they *are* out to get you.

The Republican War on Science is a good read, and not just because I quite *like* a little hyperventilation.

I've read reviews that accuse Mooney of polemic; some seriously, polemically negative reviews.[1] I don't care to reheat that. I think such criticism is misplaced. Still, a potboiling polemical style will *deform* presentation in predictable ways, leading to these sorts of misunderstandings. Let's consider.

First, there is concern about choir-preaching. Consider THE RECENT PEW RESEARCH CENTER REPORT that found, among other things, that substantial numbers of Republicans are so-called Enterprisers: "The staunchly conservative Enterprisers have perhaps the most consistent ideological profile of any group in the typology. They are highly patriotic and strongly pro-business, oppose social welfare and overwhelmingly support an assertive foreign policy. This group is largely white, well-educated, affluent and male—more than three-quarters are men. While Enterprisers are a bit less religious than the other GOP groups, they are socially conservative in most respects." What you've got here is your basic Newt Gingrich—to a lesser extent, your Glenn Reynolds, Tech Central Station-type. Being pro-science is, on average, part of your self-conception if you are an 'enterpriser'. You are an optimistic believer in the power of technology and science to generate wealth and improve human life. This lot will look at Mooney's cover and feel personally slandered. 'How can *I* be part of a war on science? I think the X-Prize is *great*! I want science to make me live forever! I *love* my new digital camera! *Liberals* are the ones who are always refusing to look at the facts. Look what they did to poor Larry Summers because he tried to speak truth to power! They buried their heads in the sand when *The Bell Curve* came out! Whimpering about 'frankenfood'. Postmodern nonsense! What the academy needs is a return to reason! They're arrogant and elitist and they want to cram their lefty values down everyone's throats, packaged as 'science'! (Like that smug scientist bastard in *The Day The Earth Stood Still*, who helped the alien turn everyone's cars off to teach them a lesson. *That's* academic science for you. Telling everyone how to live their lives.)'

However many grains of truth you think you see in this heap, it's clear there will be enough sand in some eyes to keep *War on Science* from a fully considerate reception. I don't want to be naive and say: if only you reasoned with them in a friendly, respectful way, you could make them see. One of the things the Pew research shows is that this lot is ideologically consistent, which suggests a certain partisan hardening. They won't peel easy. The more libertarian ones will stick with 'POX ON BOTH YOUR HOUSES.' Still, one ought to try. At any rate, a less polemical performance of the thesis is worth rehearsing if only to the choir. (Not that you can't sing the other version. There are actually good reasons to have two versions.)

'War on science'. I'm guessing that was marketing's idea. The notion is suggestive of the absurd. A meeting of the cabal:

ID-supporter (Ned Flanders) and 'sound science' industry apologist (Homer hired as a flack). Roll clip of Homer and Lisa debating on Kent Brockman's show. Lisa is cut off before she can finish. "Well, the only reasonable thing to conclude is that you're both half right. And that's my two cents." Monty Burns explains that he paid to have Lisa's school report on nuclear waste trashed not because the truth would have cost him millions but because there's a war on science: "We must prevail, because—so it has been written—against stupidity, even the Gods must strive in vail. These Democrats, gentlemen, are no Gods! To ignorance! TO IGNORANCE!" Professor Frink suddenly falls through the skylight: "ah, with the biasing and the fringe sciencing and the phony journalistic balancizing ba-*hey!*"

(Mooney knows I'm laughing *with* him. I *like* his book.) Anyway, being anti-science is not anyone's idea of an end, with respect to which individual acts of stupidity are perpetrated as calculated means. Mooney never says otherwise. But, preoccupied with bringing our indignation to a steady boil, he does not lay out, clearly and comprehensively, exactly what he thinks instead of any silly conspiracy theory. He quotes the Union of Concerned Scientists on misrepresentations, suppressions and sundry tamperings (p. 238): "Other administrations have, on occasion, engaged in such practices, but not so systematically nor on so wide a front." Grant the wide front (I do, and not just for the sake of argument); the systematicity is still a BIG question-mark. Is the claim really that the corruption is qualitatively different, i.e. more 'systematic', in addition to just plain being *more*? Or is the charge just that there is a bigger pile because it's a bigger elephant (because it certainly has grown.)

The book concludes:

> This political movement has patently demonstrated that it will not defend the integrity of science in any case in which science runs afoul

of its core political constituencies. In so doing,
it has ceded any right to govern a technologi-
cally advanced and sophisticated nation. Our
future relies on our intelligence but today's
Right—failing to grasp this fact in virtually every political situation in which it really matters,
and nourishing disturbing anti-intellectual tendencies—cannot deliver us there successfully or
safely. If it will not come to its senses, we must
cast it aside. (p. 269)

The first sentence says it: there *isn't* a war on science. Science is collateral damage in a driveby shooting aimed at ...
what? What way is it science gets in, and why? I should stop
right here, for I am no science journalist like Mooney. Nevertheless, a few suggestions. Obviously I'm inducting from
the data set Mooney himself has provided. (Really, it's a *great*
read.) Obviously Mooney sees perfectly well what I am suggesting. But I feel that ... well, the polemic prevents Mooney's
own pretty clear implications from getting expressed with
sufficient analytic clarity. Getting clear is both important in
itself, and probably genuinely important for purposes of converting at least a few on the other side.

Chris Mooney is not made of stone, so he helps himself to
the most delicious slice of sweet philosophic stupidity served
up, lo these past six years. The 'reality-based community'
thing from the 'senior advisor' to the President quoted in the
2004 Ron Susskind *NY Times* article:

The aide said that guys like me were "in what
we call the reality-based community," which
he defined as people who believe that solutions
emerge from your judicious study of discernible reality." I nodded and mumbled something
about enlightenment principles and empiricism.
He cut me off. "That's not the way the world

really works anymore," he continued. "We're
an empire now, and when we act, we create our
own reality." (quoted, p. 257)

And so we have gotten (genuinely funny) jokes about the
'postmodern presidency'. I've done a spot of that myself. Kidding aside: with these folks we've got a compound of Machiavellianism, zealotry, and—in foreign policy matters—hubris.
That last ingredient may presently be evaporating upon contact with reality. At any rate, let's consider Machiavellianism
and zealotry. We know what this is. It's clear that sometimes
ignoring facts—lying—can be shrewd. You know what you
want. An inconvenient fact obtrudes. Ignoring it, blowing past
it, may work. First, if you suspect those who unearthed the
fact are your political enemies, they may be coloring things in
to suit their ends and values, so you may as a matter of heuristic strategy opt always to lean the other way. Second, someone may find a solution to the problem later—happens all the
time in science. Third, by the time it gets really bad it may
be someone else's problem. Or at least you will have enough
power not to take responsibility. Zealotry compounds this.
Machiavellians on a mission from God are exemplary when
it comes to ignoring inconvenient truths. There is not much
mystery in the fact that such personality types *can* thrive in
politics. And *there* you have the Bush/Rove problem. But why
pin it on Republicans generally? Well, yes, they have to take
responsibility for Bush. But beyond that, is there something
about the current system, the specific nexus of politics and
policy and science that obtains at present, that *especially* selects for this type? If so, has this system arisen by accident or
design?

Obviously in the past it has been the case that some on
the left sacrificed science to political values—or at least to
specific goals. Mooney himself mentions Lysenko. There you
go. Zealous leftists are capable of disregarding, of being blindly arrogant, etc. Activists, reformers, revolutionaries on both

wings tend to get tired of 'it'll never work', because they feel this is almost always a lazy excuse for not trying, or just a straightforward attempt to block what is properly an argument about ends. So they tune out skepticism, often with disastrous results. Technocratic consent-manufacturers smuggle values into findings, disguised as facts, feeling it is at once their duty and privilege to impose values on others. Of course the line on the right is to claim that this is what we have in fact got—entrenched, detached, arrogant academic elitists. This is not plausible, mind you, but protesting the very notion will fail to convince. Let me quote another bit from Mooney:

> Testifying before a National Academy of Science panel in July 2004, Michigan Republican congressman Vernon Ehlers, himself a physicist and generally regarded as a champion of science, defended the practice of asking advisory committee appointees about their voting records and party affiliation. "I think it's an appropriate question. I don't think scientists should consider themselves a privileged class—that politics is for everyone else and not for them," Ehlers stated, In effect, he blessed the notion of dividing science into "Republican" and "Democratic" camps. (To some extent, scientists may well divide this way, but there is no reason to make matters worse.)
>
> When the National Academy released its final report, it unequivocally rejected Ehler's position. "It is no more appropriate to ask S&T [science & technology] experts to provide non-relevant information—such as voting record, political-party affiliation, or position on particular policies—than to ask them other personal immaterial information, such as hair color or height," wrote the committee. But the damage

had been done. A prominent Republican *and scientist* had taken a stance in favor of science politicization to defend the administration. . . . (p. 258)

Mooney, following the National Academy statement, protests too much. Ehlers looks to be engaged in partisan watercarrying. But—as Mooney himself says at other points—it's unrealistic to think partisan affiliation is as irrelevant as, say, hair color. Mooney would be suspicious of a scientific committee that found in favor of policies favored by Republicans, which turned out to be stacked with Republicans. That would send up a little warning flag. Mooney advocates full-disclosure in 'science court' cases. "Congress should implement mechanisms to ensure full disclosure of any potentially relevant conflict of interests by witnesses invited to testify at hearings at the time of their testimony. such a step would at least partially deter the worst excesses of the "science court" tradition" (p. 264). Obviously an apologist for these courts might say: 'scientists may indeed divide between 'industry-friendly' and not. But there is no need to make matters worse by dragging this fact into the light.' Well, the goose-gander concern is clear enough. Even if they are engaged in a bit of partisan maneuvering, there is every reason to think that the likes of Ehlers seriously think full partisan disclosure would be a salutary 'sunlight' measure.

Let me conclude by modestly suggesting that what is needed is a more explanatory argument for the systematic inferiority of the Republican party on science matters. This needs to take seriously, if only hypothetically, the view that right partisanship just balances out left partisanship. The way to rebut this line is to specify and document systematic tendencies on the right which are absent, or less present, on the left, and which are not counterbalanced by any uniquely leftish bad tendency. There are, by my count, really just two major candidate factors: culture war and corruption by deep-pocketed industries/corporations. The right has a significant constituency that is not exactly anti-science, but gratified by a sense of science as culturally subordinate to Christianity. Fights over evolution are about *pride*. But this *starts* on the right. The blogosphere's most stalwart ID scourge, PZ MYERS, didn't go into biology to fight ID'ers. But the ID'ers definitely went into biology to achieve a sense of superiority over the likes of PZ. All the same, there is a certain tokenism to this culture war. Science must be compelled to bend the knee on a few public occasions. But everyone knows science makes DVD players. We *want* those. Attacks on science on the cultural front are never going to go too far. As annoyed as PZ is by the ID'ers, I suspect that straightforward corruption is the much bigger ticket item. If it is possible to buy *scientific* influence; if politicians can cherry-pick scientific 'results'; then money can buy facts. Certain sorts of facts (or their suppression) are so valuable that they will be bought if they can be. Republicans are the party of business, so they will be disproportionately corrupted. There is no way to 'privatize' this sort of scientific inquiry so that the profit motive follows finding truth, rather than pleasing those willing to pay for certain truths. So gung-ho X-Prize boosterism as a model of how science should be done doesn't fly in these contexts. (Please note: this is not an argument, it is an outline of an argument.) So then you have, not a 'war on science' but a money-trail, leading to a 'science sold to the highest bidder' model.

What I want is for Mooney to present a polemic-free version of his thesis, just to get clear about these things.

▼

And that's where my original piece stopped. I've edited it, mostly for clarity. Chris responded—not fully, but I *did* basically ask him to write a new book. I wish I had made clearer that I can perfectly well see that what he writes in his response is already implied by what he wrote. The only issue is that, because it is somewhat contradicted by the rhetoric—which builds extra indignance by laying on the intentionality—the implications are never really analyzed explicitly, though they are unmissable by any moderately charitable reader. He clearly isn't a conspiracy theorist, nor a practitioner of the paranoid style, but what *other* thing he is *instead* isn't *quite* explicit enough. I ended up pushing that point to the point of demanding proof that the systematic tendencies on the Republican side will continue to be worse than any on the other side. Since that is a flagrant impossibility, I should have asked for something saner. Maybe: a rhetorically compelling response to the narrative frame invariably deployed by the other side on the science question. In his response to my post (p. 86) Mooney quotes Quiggin:

> There are few issues on which Democrats in the US, or social democrats and liberals elsewhere have taken a position that is obviously at variance with the findings of mainstream science. By contrast, there is almost no scientific discipline, from geological analysis of the age of the earth to epidemiology to climate science that has not been subject to ideological attack from Republicans and associated interests.

The problem with this is that, although plausibly true and crucial (*I* don't have a problem), it doesn't really address one of the main sources of conservative concern: trumped up social science. In my post I linked to Glenn "Instapundit" Reynolds and very next day he posted about the politics of psychology; that is, the suspicion that leftwing psychology professors dress up partisan value-judgments as empirical results. I think a big part of the response to this sort of concern should be: but this really isn't all that consequential, even if it's true that you can dig up some earnest lefty scientists engaging in it (which is plausible enough for me to grant, for the sake of the argument.) You can be annoyed this, by all means, if you are on the right. You can criticize it. But at the end of the day it's small potatos, in terms of its impact on policy. So you shouldn't pretend it balances out the cases Mooney discusses, which are more serious. (Again, this isn't an argument, merely a possible outline of one.)

NOTES

1. See, for example, THIS *Washington Post* review, by Keay Davidson (Sept 18, 2005): "At best, the book is a handy summary of familiar stories about the Bush administration's comic-opera style of making science policy. But the stories here seem curiously disconnected; if they're covertly linked by a systematic, subterranean Republican conspiracy against science, Mooney has failed to uncover it."

originally posted March 27th, 2006
http://crookedtimber.org/2006/03/27/mooney-minus-the-polemic/

⑦ War with the Newts

HENRY FARRELL ❱

I've already reviewed Chris' book at length (pp. 5–9), and talked there about why I liked it. What I want to do in this contribution is to develop the line I argued was missing from the book. Short version: Chris presents latterday Republican science policy as the product of an unholy alliance between big business and the religious right. He laments the powerlessness of traditional moderate Republicans who believed that science and scientific truth are good and important. This allows him to get at an awful lot of what is wrong about the Republican party's current approach to science. But it misses out on something important. There's a strand of Republican thinking—represented most prominently by Newt Gingrich and by various Republican-affiliated techno-libertarians—that has a much more complicated attitude to science. Chris more or less admits in the book that he doesn't get Newt, who on the one hand helped gut OTA (or at the very least stood passively to one side as it was gutted) but on the other hand has been a proponent of more funding for many areas of the sciences. I want to argue that getting Newt is important.

What drives Newt and people like him? Why are they so vigorously in favour of some kinds of science, and so opposed to others? The answer lies, I think, in an almost blindly optimistic set of beliefs about technology and its likely consequences when combined with individual freedom. Technology doesn't equal science of course; this viewpoint is sometimes pro-science, sometimes anti- and sometimes orthogonal to science as it's usually practiced. Combining some half-baked sociology with some half-arsed intellectual history, I want to argue that there is a pervasive strain of libertarian thought (strongly influenced by a certain kind of science fiction) that sees future technological development as likely to empower individuals, and thus as being highly attractive. When science suggests a future of limitless possibilities for individuals, people with this orientation tend to be vigorously in its favour. When, instead, science suggests that there are limits to how technology can be developed, or problems that aren't readily solved by technological means, people with this orientation tend either to discount it or to be actively hostile to it.

If poets are the unacknowledged legislators of mankind at large, science fiction authors are the legislators of modern libertarianism. Not an original point I know—it's commonly acknowledged that there's an elective affinity between a certain strain of SF and modern US style libertarianism. The two emerged in conversation with each other—the SF of A.E. van Vogt, mid to late period Heinlein and others took basic libertarian tropes, and sent them back with topspin. The individual against the state. The individual as superhuman. Space as the high frontier. An implicit faith that there's no problem out there that can't be solved by some guy with ingenuity and an engineering degree. More recently, there's Neal Stephenson, and the even more influential novels, short stories and occasional essays of Vernor Vinge, who is one of the most influential libertarian intellectuals today. (You could make a plausible case for him being *the* most influential; and, in my opinion, not undeservedly so.) Vinge's idea of the Singularity—a point in the near future at which technology accelerates out of control and the future goes non-linear—has been taken up with gusto by SF authors. The predicted future in which we all upload to computers, go posthuman or whatever, has been unkindly described as the Rapture of the Nerds by Ken

MacLeod. But it provides some powerfully attractive ideas and metaphors for libertarians—specifically, ideas about and metaphors of how technology can crush bureaucracies and liberate the individual. It also represents a kind of pure distillation of a particular set of libertarian myths, in which new technology serves as a kind of MAGICAL PIXIE DUST that dissolves complicated political, social and environmental problems into nothingness.

Take as Exhibit One, Glenn Reynolds' recent book, *An Army of Davids*, in which home brewing merges into DIY teddybear construction into blogging into nanotechnology into individual powered spaceflight and it all gloms together with the Singularity. If there's a connecting thread in the book (and it's a pretty weak thread at times), it's an argument that technology is leading to a radical widening of individual choices. What is interesting to me about this is the underlying vision of technology and politics that this book (and other books and articles like it) represent. On the one hand, it's not anti-science. Glenn can't wait for this brave new world to come into being; he's quite convinced that he and home-recording ballista-building machine-gun toting wargamers everywhere are going to do pretty well in it. Blessed are the geeks, for they shall inherit the earth. He's vigorously in favour of stem cells, nanotechnology, and a *laissez faire* attitude to scientific research in general. But there's also something a little weird about his enthusiasm. It's less an excitement about science as such than about technology, or for that subset of scientific speculation and facts which suggest that there aren't any fundamental limits to human ingenuity. Scientific results which suggest that there are such limits don't seem to make it through his filter.

Take as Exhibit Two, TECH CENTRAL STATION. As Chris and others have documented, it's a shill website, run by a crowd of corporate lobbyists to push articles that favour their interests. Less Tech than Flack. But there's still, if not an ethos there, at least a carefully burnished PR image that runs through its pieces, an idea of technology, libertarian economics and free markets combining to free the individual, all provided that evil government bureaucrats aren't allowed to interfere. The site has a certain appeal because of this image—without a spuriously independent organizing myth of this sort, it probably wouldn't be worth its funders' money and time. It suggests a certain vision of the future, which may in practice be anti-science much of the time (at least when science comes into conflict with corporate interests), but which doesn't sound anti-scientific.

Take, finally, Newt Gingrich himself. On the one hand, enthusiastic for technological development, and indeed for more funding for the sciences; on the other, a keen proponent of the Strategic Defense Initiative, which got written into the Contract with America under his watch, despite the consensus among a large number of serious scientists that the program was simply unworkable (I suspect that the Star Wars program serves as a kind of litmus test for the subset of techno libertarians that I'm writing about; if you're one of them, you were and probably are still for it.) Newt is almost a paradigmatic example of the technology geek unleashed on politics, with fascinating albeit frequently awful results. (Newt may be quite crazed, but one gets the sense that he'd be interesting to talk to, in a way that, say, Tom DeLay would not.)

I reckon that there are important lessons to be learned here which don't emerge from Chris's book. First, that there is a segment of the Republican party, which isn't moderate in the traditional sense of the term, but which pro-science lefties can strike alliances with on a specific subset of scientific issues. To take one example, Glenn Reynolds has, in fairness, made visible his disdain for Republican posturing on stem cell issues. To the extent that the Christian right wants to impede this or that aspect of scientific research, which it sees as interfering with God's plan, there's probably a natural commonality of interests that can be appealed to. Many techno-libertarians may not be especially reliable allies, but to the extent that many of them do take their beliefs seriously, they're likely to resist restrictions on contraception and reproductive technologies, on genetic research and related issue areas. By the same token, they're obviously likely to be on the other side when the issues involved are government regulation on environmental or health issues that arguably impinge on individual freedom.

Second, if you want to take seriously the threat posed by organizations such as Tech Central Station (which doesn't seem to me to be sincerely committed to techno-libertarianism, but which is certainly willing to use techno-libertarian language to mask corporate interests), you have to recognize that part of their power to persuade is that they seem as though they're committed to the development of exciting new technologies. When one wants to take on politicians like Newt who want to revive massively expensive programs for missile defense that don't make sense in terms of basic science, one has to recognize that a large part of these programs' appeal is that they sound scientific. Indeed, they appeal to a set of myths that American scientists themselves helped to build and propagate during the Cold War in order to win resources. They haven't been successful only because they've taught 'the controversy' but because they've also stolen some of the clothes of those they want to displace. Which makes the task of separating them out from genuine voices in the debate that much more complicated.

originally posted March 27th, 2006
http://crookedtimber.org/2006/03/27/war-with-the-newts/

⑧ The War and the Quarrels

Tim Lambert ▶

Readers of my ʙʟᴏɢ will know that I have written about some
of the same issues that Mooney describes in *The Republican War
on Science*. For example, the way tobacco companies used groups
they secretly funded to lobby epidemiologists to adopt "Gᴏᴏᴅ
Eᴘɪᴅᴇᴍɪᴏʟᴏɢʏ Pʀᴀᴄᴛɪᴄᴇs," "Practices" that would rule out
finding second-hand smoke to be harmful. So I certainly agree
that there is some sort of war on science going on, and I can vouch
for the accuracy of Mooney's book on the topics that I have also
researched. What I am concerned about is the other part of the
title: "Republican". Is that justified? Are the Republicans the
only ones making significant attacks on science?

The title put me in mind of a book from the 1990s: *Higher
Superstition: The Academic Left and Its Quarrels with Science*, by
Gross and Levitt.

They identified a different group as being against science,
the ᴘᴏsᴛᴍᴏᴅᴇʀɴ "academic left", which doesn't seem to intersect much with Republicans. Are Mooney and Gross and Levitt
just ignoring attacks on science from outside the groups they
identified?

First, Gross and Levitt's target, the postmodernists—Mooney
ignores them. I think that is interesting because he doesn't ignore the left-wing abuse of science from opponents of geneti-
cally-modified organisms and animal rights activists. And he
talked to plenty of scientists, so it seems that scientists don't

feel themselves under attack from the postmodernists any more. Still, it would have been worthwhile drawing out the connections with the other attacks on science. For example, the tobacco companies' approach to "Good Epidemiology Practices" seems pretty postmodern—they felt they could get the rules of science changed by lobbying scientists the same way they lobbied lawmakers.

Next, the Creationists. Gross and Levitt ignore them, though Gross went on to help write CREATIONISM'S TROJAN HORSE: THE WEDGE OF INTELLIGENT DESIGN, while Levitt BLAMES POMO for softening up intellectuals for the attack of the creationists.

Last, the anti-environmentalists. Here the two books intersect in the person of Dixy Lee Ray in *Trashing the Planet*, who made several pseudo-scientific arguments against ozone depletion. For example, (and people still keep bringing it up) "volcanoes put more chlorine into the stratosphere than CFCs" (debunked HERE if you are interested). Mooney shows how Sherwood Rowland debunked Ray's argument and documents how despite this, Republicans used Dixy Lee Ray's volcanoes to push for a repeal of restrictions on CFCs. On the other hand, Gross and Levitt recommend *Trashing the Planet* and describe Dixy Lee Ray as "straight-shooting." And they must surely have known that her volcano theory was completely bogus because they concede that CFCs cause ozone depletion, citing an article by Gary Taubes that specifically debunks her volcano theory.

I believe that Gross and Levitt damaged their credibility by ignoring and endorsing right-wing attacks on science. I don't think that is true about Mooney, but it still would have been better to devote more space to describing the left-wing attacks on science.

NOTES

I learned about Ray and Taubes and Gross and Levitt from Jeff Shallit's REVIEW of *Higher Superstition*.

originally posted on March 27th, 2006
http://crookedtimber.org/2006/03/27/the-war-and-the-quarrels

⑨ If There's a War, Please Direct Me to the Battlefield

STEVE FULLER ▶

Perhaps authors should not be judged by the quality of insight expressed in their epigraphs. But were one so inclined, one would have to conclude that Chris Mooney is profoundly naive about how science works. Indeed, he displays a level of naiveté about the sociology of science unbecoming in any other field of journalistic inquiry. (He may need my course on the 'EPISTEMOLOGY OF JOURNALISM'!) Readers of *The Republican War on Science* are initially regaled with an epigraph from Steven Pinker, the first sentence of which reads:

> The success of science depends on an apparatus
> of democratic adjudication—anonymous peer
> review, open debate, the fact that a graduate
> student can criticize a tenured professor.

The pages that follow clearly indicate that Mooney believes not merely that this is a normative ideal toward which science as a whole aspires or to which pieces of scientific research might be, in principle, held accountable. Were either the case, I would be on side with him. Unfortunately Mooney also seems to believe that science is *normally* conducted this way. Journalists, if anyone, should be scrupulous about distinguishing what people do from what they say they do. The ethnographic methods so beloved in the more qualitative reaches of social science are historically indebted to just such first-hand coverage of previously neglected features of the life circumstances of workers and immigrants in the late 19th and early 20th centuries. However, Mooney's trust in the peer review system is based purely on high-minded hearsay. So let me report briefly as an 'insider' to the process.

The only place a graduate student is likely to criticize a tenured professor—and live to fight another day—is an elite university, especially when the professor speaks outside his expertise (as Pinker often does). Moreover, this phenomenon bears no relation to the workings of the peer review process used to decide grants and publications. Contrary to the democratic image that talk of 'peerage' connotes, relatively few contributors to any science are regularly involved in the process. For the most part, there are no conspiracies here. It is simply a pain to spend time evaluating someone else's work when you could be doing your own work. Peer reviewing is a mark of 'good citizenship', a euphemism for sacrificing a bit of yourself for the collective enterprise to which you would contribute. There are rarely any formal incentives to participate in the process. Of course, if you work in the same field, the burden is eased—but then ethical issues arise: Will you stymie your peer's publication so that you can be on record as having said something similar earlier? In any case, funding agencies and academic editors tend to gravitate to a relatively small set of referees who exhibit both reliability and soundness of judgement. While this process may resemble capitalism's 'invisible hand', it is hard to see how it would conform to any reasonable understanding of 'democracy'. It is surprising Mooney trusts Pinker as a source for the virtues of the peer review process, since Pinker's last four books, all best-sellers, have been with commercial publishers.

Science journalists are more like philosophers of science than either probably care to admit. Both are involved in public relations work for science without pretending to be scientists themselves. Of course, journalists and philosophers differ in deadline pressures, but they are similar in structuring their narratives around events, ideally ones where a discovery precipitates a decision with momentous consequences for an entire line of inquiry. Who exactly makes the 'discovery' is an interesting question, since it need not always be the scientists themselves. It could be the journalist or philosopher, who realizes that a specific moment marks a turning point in a heretofore open-ended situation. Much depends on how the event is framed: what exactly is 'news' here? For example, what was newsworthy about the mapping of the human genome—that it was done at all or that it was the outcome of a race between a publicly and a privately motivated team, or perhaps that both teams 'won' on their own terms?

That many—perhaps most—would regard the bare fact that the human genome was mapped as news indicates just how little the general public previously knew about how much scientists know about our genetic makeup. From a strictly scientific standpoint, mapping—or, more precisely, sequencing—the human genome was little more than an industrial application. The only problems concerned the efficiency of the mapping. That a public and a private team competed to map the genome speaks to the anticipated consequences for the biomedical sciences and biotechnology: There is potentially huge consumer value in the mapping, but who will pay for what to be done? Perhaps that is a more newsworthy item. But one might equally argue that the segmentation of the scientific reward system, whereby one team gets its intellectual property rights and the other its Nobel Prize, points to the deepest issue of all, one that threatens any unity of purpose that scientific inquiry might be thought to have.

The question of intellectual integrity in both the journalistic and philosophical cases pertains to just how independent your representation of science is. Are you doing something other than writing glorified press releases for thinly veiled clients? It must be possible to be pro-science without simply capitulating to the consensus of significant scientific opinion. With this in mind, I am struck by Chris Mooney's professed journalistic method:

> Let me explain my principles for reporting on science. In my opinion, far too many journalists deem themselves qualified to make scientific pronouncements in controversial areas, and frequently in support of fringe positions. In contrast, I believe that journalists, when approaching scientific controversies, should use their judgment to evaluate the credibility of different sides and to discern where scientists think the weight of evidence lies, without presuming to critically evaluate the science on their own. (p. xv)

The rhetoric of this statement is a marvel to behold. Mooney begins by distancing himself from colleagues who think they can pronounce on scientific debates. So, it would seem, Mooney defers to scientists. However, his own stated policy is 'to evaluate the credibility of different sides', which sounds a lot like constructing an independent standpoint from which to pronounce on scientific debates. Mooney may be caught here in a contradiction of purpose, but I might applaud the latter purpose as befitting a journalist who aspired to be the Walter Lippmann of the science field. Unfortunately, in the same sentence, Mooney dashes this hope by cashing out his idea of 'evaluation' in terms of simply reporting the considered opinion of scientists.

Now, even this would not be so bad if Mooney had an independent way of gauging scientific opinion. But alas, he does not. Most of *The Republican War of Science* is about self-identified armies of scientists and policymakers. This is very much of a piece with the elite nature of political struggles in modern complex democracies. Nevertheless, these elites are a fraction of all the people whose cooperation is necessary for any policy to take effect. Mooney's oversight, which admittedly is characteristic of most contemporary science journalism, would never happen in political journalism. Imagine a journalist covering an election who reported the opinions of candidates and party operatives, and then turned only to think-tanks for assessments of the merits of the party platforms: No public opinion polls to establish the breadth and depth of voter sympathies. No probing interviews about which campaign issues really matter to voters. The natural conclusion to reach is that such a journalist has allowed herself to be drawn into the vortices of the spin doctors, whose combined judgments may or may not bear some resemblance to the election outcome.

For example, Mooney takes the judgement of the National Academy of Sciences (NAS) as the gold standard of scientific authority. Yet, it is nothing but a think-tank that Abraham Lincoln created to provide advice during the Civil War, which has been increasingly called upon by various branches of the federal government to research and advise on science-based policy issues. It is a self-selecting and self-perpetuating body of advisors that is not accountable to the rank-and-file of the scientific community, let alone the electorate at large. To be sure, NAS members are typically very accomplished scientists. But it is not clear that the quality of a scientist's judgment is improved as her achievements are rewarded. On the contrary, both the rewarding community and the rewarded scientist may come to adopt a superstitious attitude toward everything the scientist thinks. The rewarders confer a halo effect on the rewarded, a compliment the rewarded return by mounting scientific hobby horses that threaten to distort science's overall research agenda.

A notable case in recent memory is the ill-fated Superconducting Supercollider, a Congressionally funded project to build the world's largest particle accelerator in Texas. It is conspicuous by its absence from *The Republican War on Science*, though its heyday occurred during a Republican presidency, that of the first George Bush. The NAS was strongly behind it, fronted by distinguished physicists like Steven Weinberg and George Smoot. The latter's work on cosmic background radiation (a key to understanding the aftermath of the Big Bang) was indebted to a satellite launched by NASA, another of the NAS's ongoing interests. This is clearly science done mainly by and for its elite practitioners who then gesture to its larger 'cultural value' to justify its support. Scientific elites, especially in physics, have adopted this bread-and-circuses approach to rebrand the grounds on which they were given *carte blanche* in the Cold War era. As should now be clear in retrospect, the 'Cold' of the Cold War referred to the intellect, rather than the body, as the terms with which the Americans engaged in conflict with the Soviets: larger particle accelerators demonstrated the nation's capacity to harness energy to deliver larger weapon payloads; longer space voyages demonstrated the nation's capacity to, if not outright colonize, survey extraterrestrial domains. In the postwar thaw, these deferred preparations for war against a foreign foe were redeployed for a more direct national conquest of the structure of reality itself. For scientists like Weinberg and Smoot, that was the whole point of the exercise all along.

There is no doubt that the Supercollider would have—and NASA has—produced good science. Indeed, good science can be produced about infinitely many things but budgets are limited and hence priorities needed. A science journalist should be sufficiently alive to this point to report consistently the likely beneficiaries and opportunity costs of alternative science funding streams. Much too often, Mooney writes as if the entire scientific community would benefit from one funding stream, while only pseudoscientists and their political mouthpieces would benefit from another. Then those falling into the latter category are formally identified and, where possible, the patronage trail is charted. Were Mooney more sensitive to the institutionalisation of science policy, he would have recognized the asymmetry of his practice. More specifically, he would have realized that two federal science policy bodies he holds in high esteem—the NAS and the erstwhile research arm of the US Congress, the Office of Technology Assessment (OTA)—operated under quite different principles, which came to the fore in the debates that eventuated in the termination of the Supercollider.

The OTA, staffed by social scientists, tended to frame analyses of the science policy environment in terms of a comprehensive statistical representation of the range of constituencies relevant to the policy issue: that is, including not only elite but also more ordinary scientists. On that basis, the OTA suggested that if the research interests of all practicing physicists are counted equally, then the Supercollider should not rank in the top tier of science funding priorities because relatively few physicists would actually benefit from it. I say 'suggested' because, whereas the NAS typically offers pointed advice as might be expected of a special interest group, the OTA typically laid out various courses of action with their anticipated consequences. My guess is that Mooney fails to mention this chapter in the OTA's short but glorious history because it helped to trigger the ongoing Science Wars, which—at least in Steven Weinberg's mind—was led by science's 'cultural adversaries', some of whom staffed the OTA, whose findings contributed to the Congressional momentum to pull the plug on the overspending Supercollider. Although Mooney is right that both the NAS and OTA have often found themselves on the losing side in the war for influence in Washington science policy over the past quarter-century, their *modus operandi* are radically different. According to the NAS, science is run as an oligarchy of elite practitioners who dictate to the rest; according to the OTA, it is run as a democracy of everyone employed in scientific research.

I have no doubt that Republican politicians have tried to commandeer the scientific agenda for their own ends—indeed, ends which, generally speaking, I oppose just as much as Mooney does. Nevertheless, there are two countervailing considerations. First, like it or not, politicians and not scientists are the chosen representatives of the people. And, at least in the US, the ballot box more reliably removes suboptimal politicians than peer review identifies suboptimal science. Second, even the most competent scientists have rarely agreed on policy direction. While I bemoan this fact just as much as Mooney would (if he knew it), to believe otherwise is simply wishful thinking born of nostalgia for Cold War science policy.

First, the politicians are accountable to specific constituencies in a way scientists, especially elite ones, never are. Politicians are ultimately in the business of promoting the public interest, and everything—including science—is a means to that end. Whether she decides to listen to the NAS or scientists aligned with industry lobbyists, a politician's fate is sealed in the ballot box of the next election. If a great many politicians who spurn the NAS win re-election, then the problem would seem lie with the disgruntled scientists rather than the politicians. Perhaps voters are happy to take risks that scientists find unacceptable. Indeed, perhaps voters are happy to remain ignorant about the exact risks because of goods that can be plausibly delivered in the short term.

Suppose either or both of these speculations is correct. Does this demonstrate the irrationality of the American public? Mooney himself prefers to point to the ignorance and duplicity of politicians, as if the citizenry, 'properly' informed, would reach conclusions that coincide with those of the NAS. (A philosopher of science, Phillip Kitcher, has indulged this fantasy as the idea of 'well-ordered science'.) Either Mooney is being incredibly polite here or he simply hasn't thought through the implications of his argument. Why doesn't he argue that a body like the NAS should function as a second Supreme Court, with the right of judicial review over federal legislation? After all, if US policymaking is really drowning in so much bad science, then wouldn't it make sense to suspend some democratic control over the research (and teaching) agenda? In Mooney's depiction, the pervasiveness of the problem certainly rivals that which brought a cabinet-level Department of Homeland Security into existence!

My own heretical view of this situation is that even if US policymakers are influenced by a degraded form of science policy, it may matter much less than Mooney thinks because the checks and balances of the political system ensures that the potentially worst effects of such policy—just like the potentially best effects of excellent science policy—are attenuated in its many stages of implementation and administration. And if this is not enough, there is always the ballot box as the site of revenge on politicians who too closely aligned themselves with a failed science policy. A historical reality check is useful here. Like so many others who fret over the current state of science, Mooney compares the Republican politicisation of science with Lysenkoism, the doomed Soviet agricultural policy based on a version of Neo-Lamarckian genetics that comported with the ideology of dialectical materialism but not with the facts of heredity. And like so many others before him, Mooney makes the mistake of concluding that the main problem with Lysenkoism was that it tailored science to fit a preconceived political agenda rather than allow science to speak truth to power. However, this conclusion only makes sense with 20/20 hindsight, since Lysenko and his Stalinist admirers were involved in at least as much self-deception as deception. Nevertheless, what could have been noted even at the outset—and had been noted by consistent opponents like Michael Polanyi—was that the Soviet science system did not permit the fair testing of Lysenkoist knowledge claims.

It is disingenuous to think that science policies will not have elective affinities with the interests of the dominant political party. Mooney admits as much in his close association of what he regards as good science with the interests of Democrats and moderate Republicans currently out of favour in Washington. The real question is whether a science policy, regardless of its political origins, is subjected to sufficient scrutiny on the path to mass realization. While it would be nice to require every policy to satisfy state-of-the-art tests before it is unleashed on the public, something comparable may be simulated by having the policy pass through many different sets of eyes (of, say, bureaucrats), each attuned to different interests and hence motivated to troubleshoot for different problems. And if real problems pass unnoticed, then there is always the ballot box—hopefully enhanced by the spadework of investigative science journalists!

In short, the lesson of Lysenkoism is *not* to beware the politicisation of science, but to beware the *authoritarian* politicisation of science. The *democratic* politicisation of science— of precisely the sort encouraged by the federalist construction of the US Constitution—is fine. To be sure, I don't mean to counsel a panglossian complacency toward the general state-of-affairs Mooney describes. But as it stands, it seems to me that the best course of action for those interested in improving the quality of science in policymaking is simply to try harder within the existing channels—in particular, to cultivate constituencies explicitly and not to rely on some mythical self-certifying sense of the moral or epistemic high ground. Sometimes I feel that the US scientific establishment and the Democratic Party are united in death's embrace in their failure to grasp this elementary lesson in practical politics.

This raises the second countervailing consideration: science, depending on how you look at it, is a many-splendored thing or a house divided against itself. It is not by accident that the NAS was formed during the Civil War. Warfare, in both its preparation and execution, has provided the only reliable pretext for consolidating national scientific resources, where scientists have arguably spoken in one voice. Otherwise, scientists have been loath to form representative bodies that go beyond narrow disciplinary interests, and these typically more at a national than an international level. Considering that scientific fields of inquiry have universalist aspirations, this sociological fact is striking—as well as having been an endless source of disappointment for J.D. Bernal and other Marxists who hoped that scientists could be organized worldwide to lead a proletarian revolution in the twentieth century.

Indeed, Mooney's jeremiad against the influence of scientists in the pockets of industry might best be read as evidence that scientific competence is itself no guarantee of political allegiance. This is less because scientists compromise the integrity of their expertise than their expertise is genuinely open to multiple applications and extrapolations, which may contradict each other. Whatever 'value-freedom' science enjoys lies precisely here. It arises as a by-product of the controlled settings in which scientific expertise is typically honed and tested. These always differ sufficiently from policy settings to allow for substantial disagreements. I would go so far as to suggest that much of what passes for 'data massaging', whereby empirical results are revised to justify a preferred policy option, may be explained this way. The primary sin in this case is one of omission—namely, of alternative trajectories that may be plotted from the same data, which in turn forecloses the opportunity for serious criticism of the preferred policy. The controversy over Bjørn Lomborg's *The Sceptical Environmentalist* (not mentioned by Mooney) provides an object lesson in this point.

Mooney does not take seriously that scientists whose research promotes the interests of the tobacco, chemical, pharmaceutical or biotech industries may be at least as technically competent and true to themselves as members of the NAS or left-leaning academic scientists in cognate fields. Where these two groups differ is over what they take to be the ends of science: What is knowledge for—and, given those ends, how might they best be advanced? What Mooney often decries as 'misuse' and 'abuse' of science amounts to his registering opposition to the value system in which many politicians and scientists embed scientific expertise. For example, a quick-and-dirty way to sum up the difference between scientists aligned with industrial and environmental interests is that the former are driven by *solving* and the latter by *preventing* problems. The former cling to what is increasingly called the *proactionary principle*, the latter to the more familiar *precautionary principle*.

Industry scientists function against the backdrop of an endless growth economy in which the maxim, 'Necessity is the mother of invention', is a source of inspiration not desperation. Any new product is bound to generate new problems, but those are merely opportunities for the exercise of human ingenuity—not to mention the generation of more corporate profits. That certain people are hurt by such reckless innovation must be weighed against those others who would have been hurt without it, as well as the likely costs incurred by the available policy alternatives. In contrast, environmental scientists presuppose a steady-state economy, where the ultimate concern is that our actions reflect a level of restraint compatible with maintaining a 'balance' in nature. This vision tends to privilege our current understanding of the future, including future harms, even though in the long term our understanding is itself likely to change, as we learn more. Thus, there is a risk when going down the precautionary route that the only 'steady-state' being promoted is that of our knowledge, not of reality itself, as we prevent ourselves from taking risks that might serve to expand our capacity for action. Of course, environmentalists rightly ask who has licensed industrial scientists to risk other people's lives in this fashion, which after all guarantees only profits for their paymasters and not progress for all. However, these very same critics typically would also curtail experimentation on animals for similarly risky purposes. The result looks like a fear-based policy of epistemic ossification that rivals the sort of 'faith-based' science policy that Mooney decries in creationists and intelligent design theorists.

I don't intend to resolve this conflict in scientific worldviews here. Both lay legitimate claim to advancing both science and the public interest. To be sure, the priorities of each are different, especially with respect to intertemporal issues, i.e. the relation of the short-term and the long-term. Neither world-view is especially prone to malice or incompetence, but there are clear reasons why certain constituencies might prefer one rather than the other. Moreover, the end of the Cold War has made the need for choice more evident. In my inaugural lecture as Professor of Sociology and Social Policy at Durham University in 1995, I argued that the status of science in society is shifting from that of *seculariser* to that of *secularised*: the ultimate moment of sociological reflexivity. I developed this argument in a series of works, starting with *Science* (Open University Press and University of Minnesota Press, 1997), *The Governance of Science* (Open University Press, 2000) and most recently, *The Philosophy of Science and Technology Studies* (Routledge, 2006). The basic idea is that without a state-backed unity of purpose for science, instantiated in a centralized peer-reviewed system of research funding, science is bound to gravitate in many different directions, according to the strength of competing constituencies. This is the pattern exhibited by Christianity, once the secular rulers of Europe no longer required the approval of the Roman Catholic Church. Many rival Christian churches emerged in this religious free zone, each directly appealing to people's interests, forgoing abstract arguments that in the past only served to exercise authority over those people. In such a market environment, the religious concomitant of secularisation has been evangelism.

An analogous 'science evangelism' is readily seen today in the eclipse of state-based physics-oriented research funding by client-driven biomedical research. Whereas the citizenry used to dispose of their taxes to fund science as insurance against the vague but real sense of nuclear annihilation, nowadays they conceive of science as a high-tech service customized to their wants and needs. Perhaps politicians and the general public seem so much less informed about science than ever because decisions about science are being placed more squarely in their hands. This is similar to what happened once the Bible was translated into the vulgar European languages, and believers were empowered to interpret the text for themselves. In the past, one could simply trust a state-licensed, professionally sanctioned peer review system to apply good science in a good way to good ends. People may have been just as ignorant, if not more so, but it didn't matter because they never had to take the funding decisions themselves. Like a nostalgic Catholic who in the wake of the Protestant Reformation thinks Christendom can be healed by returning to the papal fold, Mooney would have us to return to the science-authoritarian days of the Cold War, which was actually an aberration in the political history of science.

Of course, in matters of education, the scientific establishment has never had such an authoritative hold. By the standards of democracies in the developed world, the US is remarkable in lacking a national education ministry capable of enforcing uniform curricula for primary and secondary schools. Curricular guidelines are left to the states, and exactly how they are met—by what textbooks and teaching methods—is typically entrusted to local school districts. All of this is by constitutional design, reflecting the nation's founding by religious dissenters who had been disenfranchised in their native Britain. This has given the US a historic reputation for pedagogical innovation and experimentation—instances of which have been both emulated and discarded, depending on their results. However, this tendency has increasingly run up against the Constitution's First Amendment, which prevents the monopolization of public life, especially public school classrooms, by a single faith. Notwithstanding the logical leap required to move from a prevention of religious monopoly to a prevention of religious expression altogether, this has been the general course taken by the US legal system toward the inclusion of religious considerations in the science curriculum over the past eighty years, since the notorious Scopes 'Monkey Trial' over the teaching of Darwin's theory of evolution by natural selection.

Like most liberal commentators who have studied the rise of scientific creationism and intelligent design theory, Mooney can only see the hand of the religious right at work. Yet, there is more to this organized intellectual opposition to the Neo-Darwinian paradigm in biology. Let me concede at the outset some basic facts. Yes, a line of descent can be drawn from high school science textbooks espousing Biblical literalism to ones now espousing intelligent design. Yes, there is probably a strong desire, perhaps even a conspiracy, by fundamentalists to convert the US to a proper Christian polity, one that is epitomized by the notorious 'Wedge Document' (more about which below) circulating at the Discovery Institute, the Seattle-based think-tank that has become the spiritual home of anti-Darwinism. But just how seriously should these facts be taken? After all, every theory is born in an intellectual state of 'original sin', as it is actively promoted by special interests long before it is generally accepted as valid. It is therefore essential to monitor the theory's development—especially to see whether its mode of inquiry becomes dissociated from its origins. So, while intelligent design theory may appeal to those who believe in divine creation, its knowledge claims, and their evaluation, are couched in terms of laboratory experiments and probability theory that do not make any theistic references. Of course, this does not make the theory true but (so I believe) it does make it scientific.

Suppose we took the pulse of Darwinism in 1909, fifty years after the publication of *The Origin of Species* but still a quarter-century before Mendelian genetics was generally accepted as providing the mechanism for an otherwise elusive process of natural selection. We would say that the theory's main backers were located outside the universities—even outside the emerging lab-based biological sciences. To be sure, the backers were not trivial players in the knowledge politics of the day. They included popular free market intellectuals like

Herbert Spencer, as well as many 'captains of industry' whose self-understanding motivated their support of the fledgling fields of the social sciences, where 'Social Darwinism' provided a powerful explanatory and legitimatory resource for the march of capitalism.

It is common for Darwinists to airbrush away this bit of their history, which draws attention to the fact that while biologists struggled to identify the causal mechanism responsible for the striking pattern of common descent and differential evolution that Darwin recorded in nature, congenial ideological currents—including eugenics and scientific racism—kept the theory in the public eye. Thus, it is striking that the Darwin exhibition currently at the American Museum of Natural History in New York gives the misleading impression that any association between Darwin's theory and Thomas Malthus' anti-welfarist tract, *Essay on Population* is purely coincidental. Yet, Darwin himself acknowledged—and Darwin's admirers assumed—the profundity of Malthus' insight into the normal character of mass extinction, given the inevitability of resource scarcity. Contrary to the accounts usually given of Darwin's reception, what was provocative about *The Origin of Species* was not the prospect that a theory of plant and animal species could also explain humans, but the exact opposite: that a theory so obviously grounded in the explanatory framework of *laissez faire* capitalism could be generalized across all of nature. Thus, Darwin's toughest critics came from the physical and biological sciences, not the social sciences.

The ascent of Darwinism makes one wonder when the theory passed from being a well-evidenced ideology (say, like Marxism) to a properly testable science. Would it have passed the criteria used nowadays to disqualify creationism and intelligent design theory in, say, 1925, the time of the Scopes Trial? Probably not, since Darwinists still couldn't quite square their claims with cutting-edge genetics. However, it was equally clear that Darwinism enjoyed enormous support among self-styled progressive elements in American society who found lo-cally controlled school boards to be among the last bastions of intellectual backwardness. In this respect, the American Civil Liberties Union's intervention in *State of Tennessee v. John T. Scopes*, which turned it into a showcase trial, employed a more successful version of the strategy now being carried out by the Discovery Institute and other organizational vehicles for realizing the 'Wedge Document'. Just as the ACLU helped to drive a wedge between the teaching of science and theology, the Discovery Institute would now drive a wedge between the teaching of science and anti-theology, or 'methodological naturalism' as it is euphemistically called.

You would be right to suspect that I treat the two 'wedges' as morally equivalent: Both should be allowed to flourish under the aegis of American democracy. As Darwinism slowly, fitfully but finally made its way into high school and college classrooms, the theory was developed in new directions, integrated with new bodies of knowledge, virtually—but of course never quite—distancing itself from its capitalist and racist roots, especially in cognate fields like socio-biology and evolutionary psychology. I imagine a comparable fate awaits intelligent design theory over the coming decades. This prognosis requires some justification since I would be the first to admit that proponents of intelligent design theory have not always placed themselves in the best possible light. At the same time, the near-hysterical response of the Neo-Darwinist forces is itself quite revealing. Mooney reduces the entire issue to a witch hunt about whether intelligent design theory is 'really' creationism in disguise, which for him is tantamount to showing it's non-science, if not outright anti-science.

Already at this point, Mooney is guilty of two errors, one for which he cannot be held entirely responsible: he follows the baleful tendency in contemporary US legal thinking that treats 'science' and 'religion' as mutually exclusive, rather than orthogonal, categories. However, the second error goes to Mooney's journalistic acumen: instead of constructing an independent standpoint from which to evaluate scientific merits of Neo-Darwinism and intelligent design theory, Mooney's repeated practice is to ask Neo-Darwinists their opinion of work by intelligent design theorists but not vice versa. The results should surprise no one. Such opinion may indeed be expert but it is unlikely to be unprejudiced.

By the end of this witch hunt, clearly exasperated by his quarry, Mooney exclaims that Darwin's theory of evolution is 'one of the most robust theories in the history of science' (p. 190). I paused to wonder exactly what he might mean and how he might know it. It's certainly true that Darwinism has had a persistent following for nearly 150 years, regardless of its evidential support. Moreover, Darwinism is philosophically 'robust' insofar as it has caused philosophers to alter their definitions of science to accommodate a research programme that clearly does not fit the mould of Newtonian mechanics. It's also true that most practicing biologists profess a belief in Darwinism, though the impact of that belief on day-to-day empirical research is harder to establish. For example, *Science* magazine declared 2005 the Year of Evolution, but what they meant by 'evolution' relates rather loosely to what Darwin himself talked about. The magazine cited three developments: the sequencing of the chimpanzee genome, the mapping of the genetic variability of human diseases, and the emergence of a new species of bird. Only the last conforms to Darwin's own methods. Whereas he regarded natural selection as a process that occurred spontaneously in the wild and operated mainly on groups of organisms, today's breakthroughs in evolution occur mainly in the laboratory, often at the genomic or sub-genomic level, and are the product of explicit experimental interventions. That these two quite different senses of 'natural selection'—sometimes distinguished as 'macroevolution' and 'microevolution'—are seen by palaeontologists and geneticists alike as subsumed under the same 'Neo-Darwinian synthesis' is regarded by many historians as the most singular *rhetorical* achievement in science.

A good way to appreciate the intellectual challenge posed by intelligent design theory—regardless of what one makes of its origins—is to consider the rhetorical character of Neo-Darwinism. No doubt the word 'rhetorical' will seem too provocative for some readers, but it is meant quite literally. Although Darwinism starts in, say, 1860, and modern genetics is underway by, say, 1900, it is only in the period 1930-40 that the Neo-Darwinian synthesis is forged, providing the covering theory for modern biological research. The main feat, achieved most clearly by Theodosius Dobzhansky's *Genetics and the Origins of Species* in 1937, was to persuade natural historians in Darwin's research tradition and laboratory geneticists in Mendel's research tradition of a strong analogy between their methodologically rather different pursuits. In time, macroevolution and microevolution came to be understood as 'evolution' in exactly the same sense. A comparable development for some aspiring covering theory of the social sciences would be to convince, say, historical anthropologists and experimental economists that the 'markets' unearthed in the ancient world and constructed in the laboratory are to be explained by the same mechanisms, which the latter research environment reveals in their pure form. Among the obstacles to such a synthesis being forged in the social sciences include the perceived incommensurability between 'qualitative' and 'quantitative' research methods. One consequence of the Neo-Darwinian synthesis was to break down these Aristotelian hang-ups, which had also existed in biology, permitting both methods to migrate across the micro-macro divide with fruitful research results.

Thus, by no means do I wish to dismiss the Neo-Darwinian synthesis out of hand. Its construction has much to teach the social sciences, in which progress has been retarded by the sort of 'metaphysical' suspicion that Neo-Darwinism gladly suspends. Nevertheless, there remain fault lines in the synthesis, which occasionally surface, especially in the popular science literature, where the underlying assumptions and projected implications of empirical knowledge claims are discussed more openly than is normally permitted in the consensus-driven world of peer review. Mooney could have uncovered these fault lines had he asked two kinds of biologist, a field scientist and a lab scientist, what the theory of 'evolution by natural selection' is supposed to be *about*. The lab scientist would probably say that it's a model of potentially universal scope, with the actual history of life on earth as merely one—and perhaps not even the most important—confirmation of the theory. She would probably not lose too much sleep, were she to learn that natural selection proves insufficient to the task of explaining the entire history of life on earth because the model still applies in all sorts of smaller and maybe even larger domains (e.g. Lee Smolin's theory of cosmological selection). In contrast, the field scientist would turn the tables and say quite plainly that the theory of natural selection is exactly about the actual history of life on earth, and that the fate of the theory rests precisely on the extent to which it explains the patterns that Darwin and subsequent natural historians have found. Everything else is merely a metaphorical extension of the original theory.

This is quite a serious difference of opinion in how one defines a theory's referent. Perhaps, then, Neo-Darwinism is so 'robust' because it is so strategically vague—or should I say, 'adaptive'! Nevertheless, the fault lines are periodically revealed. The late Stephen Jay Gould, whose expertise was closest to Darwin's own (not least in his ignorance and disdain of lab-based science), fits my 'field scientist' to a tee. Not surprisingly, then, as the evidence from extant and extinct creatures suggested the insufficiency of natural selection as an overarching explanation for the actual history of life on earth, he became pan-Darwinism's fiercest critic. Many Neo-Darwinists have not only decried Gould's perceived defection from the fold but have more harshly criticized intelligent design theorists for trying to get some mileage from Gould's apostasy. But this is to suggest that the Neo-Darwinists have proprietary rights over the entire history of biology. Yet, Neo-Darwinism's own pivotal mechanism—what is now called 'Mendelian genetics'—was contributed by people who held the counter-Darwinian assumption that every member of a species, regardless of species history, is programmed with a reproductive propensity. That assumption is a legacy of special creationism, a research tradition in natural history that connects the devout Christians, Linnaeus, Cuvier and Mendel. To be sure, many of its elements have been subsumed by the Neo-Darwinian synthesis. But why can't intelligent design theorists reclaim this subsumed tradition as their own to develop the biological sciences in a different direction? In that case, Gould is rightly invoked as an ally—if only in a backhanded way—because he stuck to Darwin's original formulation of evolutionary theory and found it empirically wanting, whereas Neo-Darwinists have shifted the goalpost to make it seem as though the theory's validity does not rest mainly on evidence from the field.

In short, intelligent design theorists should treat what evolutionists regard as a *broadening* of their theory, which corresponds to the ascendancy of lab-based research, as involving a *thinning* of the theory's content. I was struck by this point as an expert witness for the defence in the recent *Kitzmiller v. Dover Area School District*, the first test case for the inclusion of intelligent design theory in public schools. One expert witness called by the plaintiffs, whom Mooney also quotes as a source, was Robert Pennock, my contemporary in the doctoral programme at the University of Pittsburgh's Department of History and Philosophy of Science. Pennock enthused under oath about an 'artificial life' computer programme that he and some colleagues at Michigan State University had recently written up for *Nature* magazine. To the unprejudiced observer, the programme simply looks like a strategy for generating computer viruses without the user's intervention, albeit within parameters that approximate the combinatorial tendencies of DNA. Yet, Pennock claimed that this programme 'instantiated' evolution by natural selection. The metaphysically freighted 'instantiated', much favoured by artificial life researchers, renovates the old theological idea (originally used to justify God's Trinitarian nature) that essentially the same idea can be materialised in radically different ways. Too bad, under cross examination, Pennock wasn't asked whether he thought his programme *added* to Neo-Darwinism's success at explaining the history of life on earth—or merely *substituted* for it. So much for falsifiability!

Evolutionists have been allowed to hedge their bets in this fashion because, prior to the Neo-Darwinian synthesis, there had been no 'robust' theory of the biological sciences as a whole. Biology was a scientific free zone, which is easily documented by noting the non-university locations of many of its historic practitioners. Under the circumstances, it is easy—but no less unfortunate—that a journalist like Mooney should come to make a simple equation between Neo-Darwinism and biological science as such. This leads him to suspect that intelligent design theory, which he treats alternatively as pseudoscience and antiscience, is conspiring to replace Neo-Darwinism wholesale—perhaps with some sort of Biblical fundamentalism. This really does the theory a serious injustice. At most, intelligent design theorists are guilty of opportunism, exploiting substantial differences of opinion already present in the Neo-Darwinian ranks, which the parties themselves think should be discussed in peer-reviewed publications rather than in the media, courtrooms and classrooms. Thus, intelligent design theorists typically accept exactly the sort of microevolution evidence that led *Science* to declare 2005 the Year of Evolution. But that's because 'evolution by natural selection' in these cases has been intelligently designed, namely, by the human researchers responsible for setting up the relevant experimental conditions. But what would allow natural selection to work so decisively in nature, without the presence of humans? That was the question that really interested Darwin—and Gould. It drove the analogy between 'natural selection' and 'artificial selection', which of course refers to the human breeding of animals. At this point, intelligent design theory dissents from the Neo-Darwinian orthodoxy and refuses to accept macroevolution as the final word.

Moreover, there is a *positive* programme behind intelligent design theory, though its proponents have not been as vocal about it as they might. The programme requires some imaginative thinking about 'anti-naturalism'. We need to pick up on the idea of 'instantiation' mentioned above. A scientifically tractable way of thinking about 'supernaturalism' is in terms of the same form, end or idea being realized in radically different material containers. However, some of these containers may be better suited than others for what they contain. Converting this general point into a programme of theoretical and practical problems renders 'intelligent design' scientific. (Herbert Simon's classic *The Sciences of the Artificial* can be thus read as a secular tract on intelligent design as a metatheory for all science.) Now, if we further suppose that humans have been created in the image and likeness of God—or less provocatively, that reality is in some deep way human-like— then it becomes easy to think about life itself from a design standpoint. Our technologies are then lesser versions of the divine technology responsible for all the world's creatures. By the same token, we can treat these creatures as prototypes for technologies we might develop to enhance human dominion over nature. Perhaps the most obvious of numerous historical examples is the study of birds for aviation technology. (More Unitarian Christians, like Joseph Priestley and perhaps even Isaac Newton, might say we converge with God at that point, but I offer no opinion on the matter.) In short, the biological sciences would become an advanced form of engineering, corresponding roughly to fields currently known as 'biomimetics' and 'bionics', which draw very heavily and fruitfully from contemporary biology but without any theoretical commitment to the Neo-Darwinian synthesis.

There is potentially quite a lot of money to be had by thinking of biology in this fashion, which I think helps explain why the Discovery Institute—founded as it was by technoscience sophisticates like George Gilder and Bruce Chapman—has supported intelligent design theory. To put the point bluntly, they want to corner the market on 'playing God' by both supporting the requisite technological innovations and laying down the moral ground rules for their use. Here Mooney overlooked that Gilder's 1989 bestseller *Microcosm* was one of the first books to herald the advent of nanotechnology (as 'quantum economics'). Had Mooney attended more to the continuities that have taken these young Rockefeller Republicans of late 1960s to their current support of intelligent design theory, he might have also seen the general reluctance of the Discovery Institute to be too closely aligned with genuine Biblical fundamentalists, as became clear were behind the support for intelligent design theory in the Dover school board in the *Kitzmiller* case. Indeed, it should not have been too much for Mooney to imagine that the Discovery Institute, whatever its intentions, is unlikely to succeed at spearheading some monolithic right-wing conspiracy, given that the fundamentalists who would be the foot soldiers simply want to read their biology off the Bible and not have to grapple with the scientifically informed speculations of William Dembski or Michael Behe.

The Discovery Institute is of course only one of many think-tanks trying to jump start the future of science for political advantage. Indeed, on matters relating to cutting-edge nano-, bio- and info- technology research, one might wish to turn to the judgment of such entities before that of the NAS. Of course, this is not because the NAS does not uphold good science, but simply because such an elite institution is unlikely to have its ear sufficiently close to the ground really to know what is and is not feasible in the foreseeable future, which is essential for framing any general political guidelines for research support. (That the NAS does not move very fast is symptomatic. Generally speaking, the peer review system has served to stagger publication, so as to allow a critical mass of researchers to become 'pre-acquainted' with impending research findings. But as time-to-publication shrinks in even the peer-reviewed sectors of the internet, the advantage accruing to those 'in the know' shrinks.) Imagine, if you can: What may turn out to be the best work is not being done by the 'best people' at the 'best places'! Let me make clear that I do not wish to celebrate the diffuse and largely unmonitored—and certainly unregulated—nature of emergent technoscientific trends. But we are unlikely to win Mooney's 'Republican war on science' if we cling to a nostalgic view of the authoritativeness of the self-selecting college of scientific cardinals represented by, say, the NAS.

The genius of MIT's Vice-President Vannevar Bush's *The Endless Frontier* lay in persuading postwar policymakers that the surest route to produce science in the public interest is to let scientists decide the research agenda for themselves. Not surprisingly, he made the argument turn on national security, based on the distinguished academic scientists amassed at Los Alamos who built the atomic bomb. However, an alternative framework for federal science policy had been floated even before America's entry in World War II by West Virginia Senator Harley Kilgore. He imagined a 'National Science Foundation' as an extension of FDR's New Deal. Kilgore proposed a science board in which two scientific representatives would serve alongside a representative each of labour, agriculture, industry and consumer groups.

Like most astute observers at the time, Kilgore realized that innovative scientific research in the US was being conducted off campus, as academics saddled with heavy discipline-based teaching loads were lured to informally structured interdisciplinary research parks like Bell Laboratories. He believed, I think rightly, that scientists—like other high-skilled workers—would naturally gravitate to the best labour conditions, which could eventuate in the evacuation of scientists from the public sector. Not only would it be difficult to monitor or regulate their activity, it would prove difficult to reap the benefits implied by the Constitutionally enshrined idea of science as a 'public good'. Using the Great Depression that ended the post-World War I economic boom as his benchmark, Kilgore believed that without state intervention, science would simply exacerbate class differences in American society. So, one of his many science funding schemes involved treating science education as a form of national service, whereby the government would finance the training of academically suitable students on the condition that they would spend some years developing one of America's economic backwaters.

Kilgore's relevance here is that he quite explicitly wanted to politicise science—indeed, to mount an offensive against scientists' spontaneous free market politics. Moreover, Mooney would have probably found Kilgore's politics attractive. I certainly do. Yet, Kilgore was in no doubt that good science could be done under both private and public regimes. However, by the time the vote on the establishment of the National Science Foundation reached the floor of Congress in 1950, Kilgore's proposal had come to be seen through Cold War lenses as 'politicising science' in a sense by then associated with Hitler and Stalin. Bush's victorious alternative had the federal government create a protected internal market for scientific research and later (with the launching of Sputnik) education. This has proved very costly and, not surprisingly, with the end of the Cold War, the federal government has gradually allowed science to revert to the pre-war free market state that Kilgore decried. If Mooney is genuinely interested in promoting good science in the public interest, then he needs to articulate a robust conception of the 'public interest'. The New Deal was the last time that occurred in the US outside a context of military preparedness. The legacy of that formulation is what remains of the American welfare state.

originally posted March 27, 2006
http://crookedtimber.org/2006/03/27/if-there%e2%80%99s-a-war-
please-direct-me-to-the-battlefield/

Postscript

Chris Mooney concludes the preface to the paperback edition of *The Republican War on Science* with a plea for the scientific community to engage in better public relations for their cause. Unfortunately, this is easier than done. Sometimes it is not even easily said. Mooney addresses his readers as the "reality-based community," a self-congratulatory phrase increasingly adopted by US liberals, in equal measures obnoxious and desperate—especially given that members of this community find themselves on the outside looking into the seats of real-world power.

It is worth recalling that this phrase, perhaps with a nod to the psychologist Paul Watzlawick (who, with Gregory Bateson, invented in the 'double bind' diagnosis of schizophrenia), originated in a 17 October 2004 *New York Times Magazine* piece by Ron Suskind that included the following comment attributed to an aide of George W. Bush:

> The aide said that guys like me were "in what we call the reality-based community," which he defined as people who "believe that solutions emerge from your judicious study of discernible reality." ... "That's not the way the world really works anymore," he continued. "We're an empire now, and when we act, we create our own reality [quoted to this point in Mooney, p. 257.] And while you're studying that reality—judiciously, as you will—we'll act again, creating other new realities, which you can study too, and that's how things will sort out. We're history's actors… and you, all of you, will be left to just study what we do."

In other words, the reality-based community are history's losers, the sort of people whose political imagination is likely to be fuelled by that sublimated form of resentment Nietzsche called *ressentiment*. What makes *ressentiment* trickier than ordinary resentment is that those under its spell so fully accept their own inferiority that they end up converting that inferiority into a source of strength. Thus, many of Mooney's fellow reality-based communitarians take the minority status of their common belief in evolution by natural selection to imply that the theory is much too sophisticated for ordinary folks to grasp; hence the need for better PR. (Of course, this does not explain why the US, the world's undisputed superpower in science, is one of the few countries where evolution is not widely believed.) Mooney himself is a bit more circumspect: he seems to think that people are not too dumb but too busy to worry about science policy. This then begs the question: why *should* they worry about whether evolution is the only account of the origins of life taught in high school science classes?

Mooney's concern feeds into what the astute US historian Richard Hofstadter has called 'the paranoid style in American politics'. The style is tied to the founding idea of the US as making a fresh start in the history of politics, specifically so as not to repeat the mistakes of the past, which included the establishment of a state church. American paranoia runs very deep, perhaps most viscerally in the anti-Catholicism that routinely surfaced in political campaigns until John Kennedy was elected as the first Catholic president in 1960—even though Catholicism has been the religion with the most adherents for most of American history. However, anti-religious paranoia reached a high watermark in 1987 with the Supreme Court decision in *Edwards v. Aguilard* used *motive*—as opposed to method—as the main criterion for ruling that Creationism was a religious *and not* a scientific theory. Judge John Jones had ample recourse to this precedent in his ruling against the Dover, Pennsylvania school board in December 2005, since the religious motives behind the promotion of intelligent design theory were always close to the surface.

The paranoid's fatal flaw concerns not strict accuracy but proportionality of response. Thus, Senator Joseph McCarthy may have been correct that Communists were employed by the US government in the 1950s, yet that bare fact did not justify his scare-mongering and bullying tactics, which only served to undermine the civil liberties his inquiries supposedly aimed to safeguard. Similarly, the fact that the anti-evolutionary scientific forces have been propelled by religious interests should not be sufficient to disqualify their theories from the classroom. By analogy with the McCarthy witch-hunts, more damage is done to the integrity of scientific inquiry than to its imagined opponents, who, lifted of the burden of having to defend the scientific establishment, are then free to present their challenge in the spirit of open dialogue, a.k.a. 'teaching the controversies' (which, in this Orwellian environment, is said derisorily by evolutionists).

Is there more genuine intellectual disagreement between those who do and do not take Darwin to have laid the incontrovertible foundations of modern biological science than among those who grant Darwin such an exalted status? In the current scientific cold war climate, the answer would seem to be obviously yes. However, the answer becomes less clear, once the Neo-Darwinian synthesis is seen as a relatively baggy theoretical construction, parts of which can be reasonably believed without believing the whole. It is telling that when sixty-seven national academies of science published a joint statement in June 2006 on the need to teach evolution as fact, the only beliefs clearly opposed by the agreed propositions were those of six-day creationists. For example, no appeal was made to natural selection at all, let alone as the primary explanation for evolutionary change. This was probably because the academies found natural selection a more controversial thesis than, say, that life has existed on earth for 1.4 billion years.

The airing of such thinly veiled disagreements is vital for the elaboration and development of biological science. However, this spirit is lost if 'modern evolutionary theory' (as the Neo-Darwinian synthesis is called by its proponents) must be accepted as a whole, perhaps even as a necessary condition for being taken seriously by the scientific establishment. The result, which I believe captures the current state of play in the US, distorts the intellectual horizon by minimizing differences amongst Darwinists while maximizing differences between them and their dreaded religiously inspired opponents.

A recent high-profile expression of this distortion may be found in the pages of *Intelligent Thought: Science versus the Intelligent Design Movement*, whose editor, the literary agent John Brockman, sent a copy to every member of the US Congress. The LETTER is written to whip up a McCarthy-like frenzy that no less than American economic competitiveness and national security are at risk from the promotion of intelligent design theory. Fortunately this manoeuvre has had no discernible effect on the elected officials. Meanwhile, starting in Fall 2006, at least two major British universities (Leeds and Leicester) have announced that their introductory zoology classes will devote some lectures to the controversies surrounding evolution and intelligent design.

August 23, 2006

⑩⑩ The Revolution Will Not Be Synthesized

KIERAN HEALY ▶

I am abusing my ability to post here rather than add a comment to THE ONGOING THREAD discussing Steve Fuller's response to Chris Mooney's book. I think—sorry, P.Z.—that much of what Fuller says is more or less right. To be more precise, I think the first half of his response to Mooney is pretty good, and there are some good bits later on, too. However— sorry, Steve—I also think Fuller makes an error in the way he fuses his sociology of science with his policy recommendations about what to do about the Intelligent Design movement. Moreover, he himself does the groundwork that makes the basis of the error clear. I'll try to explain.

Here's the argument. Much of what Fuller says in the first part of his post is good sociology of science. In particular, his image of science as a contested, politicized field is basically right, and—speaking as someone who believes that the present Administration is out to gut science it doesn't like—I think he's right that Chris Mooney is in danger of romanticizing the practice of science. And I agree that, at bottom, the best you can do is fight your corner. As Fuller puts it,

> It is disingenuous to think that science policies
> will not have elective affinities with the interests
> of the dominant political party... In short, the

lesson of Lysenkoism is not to beware the politicisation of science, but to beware the authoritarian politicisation of science... To be sure, I don't
mean to counsel a panglossian complacency
toward the general state-of-affairs Mooney describes. But as it stands, it seems to me that the
best course of action for those interested in improving the quality of science in policymaking
is simply to try harder within the existing channels—in particular, to cultivate constituencies
explicitly and not to rely on some mythical self-
certifying sense of the moral or epistemic high
ground. (p. 43)

Now, in my view, Fuller's contribution starts to go wrong
from about here onwards. He makes some strong points about
the messy history of Darwinian theory between the contribution of Darwin himself and the mid-twentieth century neo-
Darwinian synthesis. He then argues that the twin "wedges"
of the Scopes trial and the Discovery Institute's efforts are
"morally equivalent" and that the latter could develop in
the way that the former did. The strengths and weakness-
es of Fuller's arguments are fused together: he's at his stron-
gest when retrospectively analyzing the different ways science
might be politicized. But his argument is at its absolute weak-
est when making the case that the ID movement contains a
positive research program, in addition to being parasitic on
mainstream biology. There's little reason to believe that this
positive program is real, and—noted biologist George Gilder
notwithstanding—the only reason to think it might be is an-
alogical: the Darwinian approach did grow from a somewhat
similar social position a hundred years ago.

But this is the nub of the matter. Why should we, as more-
or-less interested actors in the field of science, let this single
consideration outweigh any others—not least the sincere belief that ID is politically motivated rubbish, for instance—to

the point that we would want to nuture ID in high schools? Early on in comments to his post, FULLER ARGUES:

> Why start teaching ID at the high school level? I received a lot publicity—and flak—for saying in the Dover trial that ID required 'affirmative action', i.e. that it could not be expected to provide a credible alternative to Neo-Darwinism without government intervention. It's clear that the few people pursuing ID openly in universities are treated as intellectual pariahs, and under those circumstances it's hard to recruit the colleagues and students needed to convert an unconventional idea into a full-fledged research programme. One solution would be to teach biology as a much more contested field, attending to the role that ID- and even special creationist thinking has contributed to what even Neo-Darwinists regard as credible science, and that the Neo-Darwinian synthesis was forged under quite specific circumstances in the 20th century.

The problem here is that Fuller has rebutted his own prescription in advance. There is no reason to believe either that "Neo-Darwinism" really needs a "credible alternative," or that ID is the entity to provide it, or that this entails that biology should be taught in high school in much the same way as the sociology of science might be taught in graduate school. As Fuller says himself, as Darwinism "slowly, fitfully but finally" established itself, it has "developed in new directions, integrated with new bodies of knowledge, virtually—but of course never quite—distancing itself from its capitalist and racist roots." In other words, while no body of knowledge is ever fully emancipated from the social conditions of its production and reproduction, modern biology's relative success in this respect means that it now sustains a wide range of alternatives to the main currents of thought in the field. So, why does it—or why do we—need ID? Not that the Discovery Institute shouldn't keep plugging away, if that's what they want. Fuller's good advice to Democrats applies directly here, too: "the best course of action for those interested in improving the quality of science in policymaking is simply to try harder within the existing channels." The ID people are entitled to do this, and they've certainly been trying hard.

They are also entitled, frankly, to be crushed like bugs in the process. Sure, they'll get control of a few school districts here and there, but—again, as Fuller says—they can be booted out later. Politically, I see no reason to support them. Scientifically, there's no compelling prospect of them being able to do anything of practical use that some better-established branch of biology can't do already. And sociologically, I don't see how Fuller's own conception of the scientific field supports the kind of "affirmative action" strategy that he advocates. Let them hammer away along with the rest of us if they like. But why should anyone care to the point of helping them out, especially when the mainstream is not, by Fuller's own arguments, all that monolithic anymore?

The question remains as to why Fuller thinks the policy he advocates is a good one (other than the hope that, if ID does win out, by the early 22nd century he might be hailed as the greatest sociologist of science in history). Maybe he's hoping for an earthquake in biology, a second modern revolution in the field. But—as Fuller surely knows—scientific revolutions of this sort cannot be willed into existence. It's not impossible that a revolution of this sort could happen—after all, Darwinism did it once already. Indeed, over the long run it's inevitable. But you can't intentionally induce this kind of revolution by means of policy or high-school curricula, for the same reason that you can't force someone to be happy or consciously will yourself to sleep. If it happens at all, it will be essentially a byproduct of other struggles—politicized, messy struggles, certainly. But while the revolution may already be brewing, you can't schedule it.

Jon Elster makes the point nicely. We'd all like to be more creative and productive, whether as artists or scientists or what have you. Maybe we'd all like a revolution in science, too. However, as Elster points out, to believe we can engineer or will this directly

> is the fallacy of striving, seeking, and searching for things that recede before the hand that reaches out for them. In many cases it takes the form of trying to get something for nothing, to acquire a character or become 'a personality' otherwise than by 'ruthless devotion to a task.' In other cases it is accompanied by self-indulgence, when one is led to tolerate errors or imperfections in one's own work because one knows they sometimes prove useful or fertile. In particular, many will have come across the brand of scientist who excuses the one-sidedness of his work by the need for fertile disagreement in science.... this attitude goes together with a form of self-monitoring whose corrosive effects I have been concerned to bring out.[1]

Science really is structured in more or less the way that Fuller describes. But for that reason, his efforts to enhance the chances of the Intelligent Design movement are most likely doomed. I can't say I'll miss them much when they're gone.

NOTES

1. Jon Elster, *Sour Grapes* (Cambridge UP, 1985), pp. 107-8.

originally posted March 28th, 2006
http://crookedtimber.org/2006/03/28/the-revolution-will-not-be-syn-
thesized/

⑪⑪ War over Science or War on Science

JOHN QUIGGIN ▶

Since my initial contribution was a fairly straightforward review, I thought I'd have another go, taking advantage of the contributions I've read.

It's pretty clear that there is some kind of war going on involving Republicans and science, but, as with Iraq, I think it's possible to distinguish two competing stories. One is that we are seeing a War over Science, considered as valuable territory. In this story Republicans like science, and particularly the technology produced by science, but would prefer a more politically reliable science that always generated the kinds of results that suit their backers.

The other is a War on Science, in the sense of an attack on the entire scientific community and their claim that scientific method is a route to knowledge that, while not infallible, is so much more reliable than any alternative as to render non-scientific approaches, such as magic, religion or rhetorical argument, irrelevant in any domain where the scientific method can be applied. Attacks on, and defences of, this claim were the central feature of the Science Wars of the 1990s.

Indeed, a striking feature of the Science Wars was the absence of a great deal of substantive concern over particular outcomes of scientific research, though there was more concern about technological applications. When the critique of the claims of science went from the general to the particular, it was quite common to see a focus on early 20th century eugenics or 19th century claims about the inferiority of women rather than on particular outcomes of contemporary scientific research.

As I read Chris Mooney, his central claim is that the War over Science, driven by the desire to get the 'right' results on issues like stem cell research, global warming, evolution and so on is being pursued with such vigour and lack of scruple as to become, inevitably a War on Science. Most of the commentators so far have suggested that Chris has been overly polemical here, and that there is a large body of people, exemplified by Newt Gingrich, who have a very positive view of science, but assume that good science must produce results favorable to their notion of individual liberty. The influence of science fiction, much of it libertarian in tone, is, as Henry points out, significant here.

I think the position is more complicated. While the Newts like an idea of science, it is not the idea associated with the scientific method, and still less with the social institutions of science: peer review, replication, formal and informal meta-analysis and so on. Just as Steve Fuller attacks these institutions from an ostensibly leftwing position, the Newts attack it from the right.

Their favored idea is that of the inspired individual genius, who sees the truth in a blinding flash of insight, and overcomes the scepticism of the mass of plodders through faith in himself (there may be female versions, but I don't recall any) and the support of a small but loyal band of followers. More or less distorted views of Galileo, Einstein and others provide the basis for this view of science, as does the vast bulk of pulp science fiction.

This model has been adopted by a string of critics of mainstream science, and of other academic disciplines. As I OB-SERVED A WHILE BACK, the pattern was set by IMMANUEL

VELIKOVSKY and has been followed by creationists, global warming 'sceptics' and so on.

As the lack of scientific support for favored Republican positions becomes more evident, we are seeing the transition from a War Over Science to a War On Science, involving attacks on the social institutions of science, including journals like *Science* and *Nature* (here's Michael Fumento at POWER-LINE), the idea of PEER REVIEW, and scientists as a group, stigmatised by Tom Bethell as a white-coated priesthood of political correctness.[1] The fact that Bethell's work is promoted by the Heritage Foundation, and that the same terms are being recirculated by the GLOBAL RIGHTWING COMMENTARI-AT is an indication that this is already a mainstream Republican position, although perhaps not yet the dominant one.

Not surprisingly, the shift to a War on Science has seen a realignment of positions from the Science Wars. The Republicans are now lining up with some of their erstwhile opponents, postmodernist and social constructivists in the humanities and social sciences, who can provide more sophisticated arguments in the War on Science than those derived from Velikovsky and his successors.

NOTES

1. Tom Bethell, *The Politically Incorrect Guide to Science* (Regnery 2005).

originally posted March 27th, 2006

http://crookedtimber.org/2006/03/27/war-over-science-or-war-on-science/

① ② Man, You Guys
Worked Me Hard . . .

CHRIS MOONEY ▶

First, I want to thank all the contributors here for launching
a very high level discussion. Because the separate commentar-
ies overlap in a number of thematic areas, they almost lend
themselves to being read in a particular order for greatest effect—and that's the sequence in which I will address them.
Here's the game plan:

First I'll touch upon what I view as the argumentative over-
view posts. Ted Barlow provides a useful and accurate review
of my book's main thesis, and then John Quiggin's first post
goes into more detail, expanding the argument's applicability
beyond the U.S. to Australia, and beyond the issues I discuss
to related ones like DDT. (Quiggin's first post also helps me
out with some of my critics, and I fully endorse his rebuttals.)
My brief reaction to these posts will comprise phase one.

Phase two: John Holbo, Daniel Davies, and Henry Farrell
dive in with thoughtful attempts to advance or reframe my
argument, or to press me on matters such as what's causing
the "war on science," whether I'm too polemical, and whether
I can account for the Newtoids or please the "Enterprisers."
This is where things start to get fun.

Phase three: Tim Lambert raises the issue of the academic
left and science, and then Steve Fuller gives us a case study in
continuing antagonisms between said academic left and the

scientific community, including the dreaded National Academy of Sciences. This part is also fun.

Phase four: John Quiggin, who somehow seems to understand my arguments even better than I do (and no, I am not being facetious), steps in to further elucidate what I'm saying. Other authors should be so lucky as to have such an apt defender. I basically agree with everything Quiggin says, so at the end I will call "tag team" and leave you in his capable hands.

With that introduction, let me discuss the entries in more detail. Ted Barlow accurately summarizes my argument when he notes of political science abusers that, "the Republican leaders in question could have made arguments for their position by arguing that moral or economic criteria sometimes trump science" (p. 12). They certainly could, and for the sake of intellectual honesty and quality of debate I wish that they would. To be fair, most of today's conservative Republicans at least try to yoke science-based argumentation to economic appeals or moral considerations. George W. Bush's early speeches on climate change, for instance, feature both a selective emphasis on scientific uncertainty and complaints about the cost of mitigation measures like Kyoto. Similarly, Bush's 2001 stem cell policy speech contained the false claim that "more than 60" embryonic stem cell lines were in existence—but it also contained plenty of moralizing. So it's not that the right doesn't make any other arguments besides scientific ones; and in fact, I suspect that conservatives often disregard expertise in economics or bioethics just as they do in science. But science gave me enough to tangle with, so I carefully limited myself to challenging specifically scientific distortions and abuses (a point that will be relevant later when I discuss Steve Fuller's post).

Moving on to the other summary-type post, John Quiggin shows that he has really gotten inside of my argument, allowing him to steer the vehicle to other locations with ease. I particularly enjoyed this comment: "The ultimate effect of the Republican strategy is to constitute a complete parallel universe, in which scientific 'knowledge' is derived from think-tanks and unqualified opinion writers rather than from actual scientists working on the topic in question" (p. 16). Exactly. This attempt to construct a conveniently walled-off alternate reality is particularly prevalent on the Christian right, whose adherents do their best to insulate themselves and their children from traditional university-based sources of scientific expertise. Not only do they flock to alternative universities like Liberty or Bryan College; they're constantly minting their own scientific "experts." Chapter 13 of my book was entitled "Sexed-Up Science," but it might just as well have been titled "Three Daves and a Joel," because it presents a kind of picture gallery of Christian right scientists who provide politically convenient arguments on emergency contraception (DAVID HAGER), adult stem cell research (DAVID PRENTICE), and the health risks of abortion (DAVID REARDON, JOEL BRIND).

Bringing up these characters, incidentally, allows me to clear up an issue that arises in John Holbo's post (and thereby transition into phase two of the discussion). That issue is intentionality. After all, political science abuse, as I've described it on the American political right, is not necessarily committed knowingly. Sometimes it is, sometimes it isn't; my sense (after going for a swim in some of the tobacco documents) is that the plotting and cynicism tend to be more prevalent on the pro-industry side of the aisle. By contrast, I have little doubt that strong Christians like the "Three Daves and a Joel" believe deeply in what they're saying. Reardon has even made a comment, quoted in my book, suggesting that since a moral God made the universe, it must operate in such a way as to lead to his particular scientific conclusions about the health risks of abortion: "Because abortion is evil, we can expect, and can even know, that it will harm those who participate in it. Nothing good comes from evil." Someone capable of making such a statement probably isn't consciously aware of conducting a "war" on science; rather, he would appear to believe (devoutly, if also conveniently) in a divinely designed world in which his conclusions must be valid by definition. But that doesn't mean no "war on science" exists: add up enough foot soldiers like the "Three Daves and a Joel" and you're sure to get one. So I continue to view the phrase "war on science" as a useful metaphor to describe the comprehensive assault upon scientific expertise across so many different areas of political salience, even if not all of these assaults are consciously intended. A "war on science" (see chapter 10)is not necessarily the goal, but it is clearly the cumulative outcome.

Holbo raises another key issue that comes up sometimes at my public talks. He's worried about the polemical packaging of my argument (which, incidentally, I do not deny). Will some people be turned off by the title *The Republican War on Science*? Undoubtedly. Last I checked there are still plenty of Republicans out there. Still, I maintain that it is an accurate title: the abuses I'm describing really have become integral to mainstream Republican political strategy. However, if we are discussing issues of tact rather than of substance, then my reply to Holbo's concern about polemicism would be the following: there are considerations of timing as well as zeitgeist to take into account. I might have written a less polemical book, and it might have been more persuasive to conservative "Enterprisers" who view themselves as pro-science (or at least to those Enterprisers who bothered to read it). But that book would not have spoken so directly to a moment in which outrage over the treatment of science by the Bush administration had reached a boiling point. There is a time for reaching out across the aisle, and there is a time for denouncing abuses in no uncertain terms. I think that we are in the latter period with respect to the treatment of science in the USA, and my tone reflects that.

But I suspect that Holbo still won't be entirely satisfied: He wants a "polemic free" version of my book, one in which I "specify and document systematic tendencies on the right which are absent, or less present, on the left, and which are not counterbalanced by uniquely leftish bad tendency." Without demanding an advance from Holbo for the new project, let me counter that I do highlight and explore these tendencies (which are generally not present on the left). They include 1) a distrust of government (which funds lots of science and uses science as a basis to regulate); 2) a general tenor of anti-intellectualism; 3) a broad distrust of universities (where much of science is conducted); 4) a strong embrace of Christian conservatism; 5) powerful pro-industry and free-market sentiment; 6) widespread proliferation of pseudo-academic (and pseudo-scientific) think tanks; and so on. These factors, when pulled together, take us pretty darn far towards understanding why the right in the US behaves in the way that it does towards science. Perhaps I don't cover all of this in enough detail for Holbo—which is fine—but on the other hand, I do seem to provide enough detail for Quiggin. Or at least so I assume, because he unintentionally answers Holbo's request with this left-vs-right comparison, which pretty much sums up my own thinking:

> There are few issues on which Democrats in the US, or social democrats and liberals elsewhere have taken a position that is obviously at variance with the findings of mainstream science. By contrast, there is almost no scientific discipline, from geological analysis of the age of the earth to epidemiology to climate science that has not been subject to ideological attack from Republicans and associated interests. (p. 14)

This makes for a good segue into Daniel Davies' helpful comments. He's right that *The Republican War On Science* is a very American book, albeit one that's had a pretty good reception in the UK (I suppose because they're so worried about us Yanks going off the deep end.) Davies says I've got the "causation wrong" in my argument, but I actually think my causal picture (which, if I could draw it, would look more like more a web of arrows than a single arrow pointing in one direction) is complex enough to accommodate Davies' comments nicely. The American "anti-intellectualism" described by Tocqueville, in its modern incarnation, is a core ingredient fueling the war on science. The same goes for what Davies depicts as a human longing after a kind of unshakeable certainty that neither science nor reality can really deliver (this, I submit, characterizes the Christian right). However, I think Davies may be underselling the power of sheer economic self-interest to explain much of what we're seeing, especially when he writes: "there is rather less obvious economic interest in trying to deny the facts about global warming...." Um, come again? Global warming exposes the dark underbelly of the entire carbon-based economy. There is therefore a huge economic stake in attacking this upstart "theory" and preserving the status quo.

Economics brings us to Henry Farrell, who gently confronts me with a couple of characters who are not the political equivalent of cardboard cut-outs and who perhaps complicate my story: Newt Gingrich, Glenn Reynolds, and maybe (I'm struggling with this one) the folks at Tech Central Station. Farrell has a lot of insight into the ideas driving this crowd, and I don't question his descriptions; in fact, I would add others, like John Tierney and Ron Bailey, to the list. And I will also admit that there is something that is at least rhetorically powerful about techno-optimism; hell, five years or so ago I was a near-convert. Finally, I will concede that the techno-optimists are great fun to make temporary allegiances with; I like to say that I agree with *Reason*'s Ron Bailey precisely half of the time.

But I'm not sure this crowd is quite as difficult for me to explain as Farrell thinks. The fact is, many of the techno-optimists are often very closely tied to industry—can anyone say Tech Central Station, or Michael Fumento's love letters to ag biotech? More generally, if it weren't for the proliferation of conservative think tanks, I doubt there would be such a chorus of techno-optimism. This helps bring the phenomenon back under the umbrella of the "war on science" thesis in the sense that it links the libertarian technophiles to one of the right's key interest groups—industry. I don't doubt that the philosophy of techno-optimism exists or that it is a firmly held view on the part of serious thinkers; but let's not forget the political mileu in which it arises.

Okay, on to phase III. Tim Lambert hits me in something of a weak spot: in the book I really ought to have discussed, at least briefly, the 1990s saga of the academic left vs. science, which has largely subsided since that time. For what it's worth, I did give my thoughts on this matter in a 2005 *American Prospect* COLUMN, wherein I pronounced the "Science Wars" of the 1990s over, having been supplanted by the dramatically more consequential "Science Wars" of the 2000s. Here's a brief excerpt:

> Even at the time [the 1990s]…the quest to root out anti-science tendencies in academia seemed a strange deployment of resources. After all, the Gingrich Republicans had just taken over Congress, set out to radically slash science budgets, and preached denial about global warming. If there was a war on science afoot, university professors probably weren't the leading culprits. Certainly they weren't the most powerful ones.
>
> Indeed, despite some undeniable academic excesses, the "science wars" were always somewhat overblown. The sociological, historical, philosophical, and cultural study of science is a very worthwhile endeavor. If scholars engaged in such research sometimes take a stance of agnosticism toward the truth claims of science, perhaps that's simply their way of remaining detached from the subject they're studying. But

it doesn't necessarily follow that these scholars are absolute relativists, to the extent of thinking that concepts like gravity are a mere matter of opinion. *Social Text* founding Editor Stanley Aronowitz has himself written that "[t]he critical theories of science do not refute the results of scientific discoveries since, say, the Copernican revolution or since Galileo's development of the telescope."

So my basic take on the "Science Wars" is that, although there might have been some genuine anti-science sentiment on the politically ineffectual academic left, the phenomenon was exaggerated and in any case, it's hardly as worrisome as a similar sentiment on the part of our actual leaders. I do thank Tim for raising the point, though. And I might add that I was unaware that Gross and Levitt, who so powerfully slammed academic leftists during the 1990s for attacking science, had promoted Dixy Lee Ray's outlandish ozone depletion contrarianism (or her book generally). If so, that's a significant hole in their pro-science armor.

But of course, there are some elements of the academic left that are actually still attacking science. Or, at least, there's Steve Fuller, CONTROVERSIAL INTELLIGENT DESIGN BOOST-ER. I don't plan on engaging with Fuller on evolution and "intelligent design"; he has taken enough licks on this subject. But let me respond to some of his other points.

Generally speaking, Fuller doesn't seem particularly concerned about correctly limning my argument; most of the times that he actually engages with me it's not the real me. Like the point about the Superconducting Supercollider—this is no gap in my account. I deliberately avoided discussing fights over how to apportion and invest research funding because they raise complicated political issues that go far beyond mere matters of distortion, suppression, and so on. And contrary to Fuller's suggestions, my descriptions of the scientific process hardly suggest someone who's sociologically naive about the matter:

> Scientists are human. They have plenty of foibles, and in some cases outright myths they tell about themselves. They also have values and agendas that factor heavily into their research decisions. Moreover, the inquiries and investigations of scientists take place in a social and cultural context that shapes both their underlying assumptions and even (at least to some extent) how they measure and interpret nature itself. (p. 14)

It may be convenient to depict me as a sociological babe-in-the-woods about science, but it wouldn't be accurate. I simply think that science matters despite its obvious shortcomings (hardly a very radical point of view). As for graduate students criticizing tenured professors, funny how that very thing just happened at the Oregon State College of Forestry. Maybe Steven Pinker wasn't so off base after all.

Moving on, I found Fuller's comparison between the Office of Technology Assessment and the National Academy of Sciences interesting, especially since he claims the OTA was staffed by "social scientists." While I'm sure there were a couple, I've met a lot of former OTA staffers, and none of them that I recall have been social scientists. Jack Gibbons, who headed the office for over a decade (and during the entire period of its significant influence), was a physicist. This is important because Fuller is trying to make the OTA appear more sophisticated than the Academy; perhaps he does he not realize that several OTA staffers went to work at the NAS when OTA disbanded.

The point is, both OTA and the NAS are needed and important institutions, and their differences are more a strength than a weakness. We need both; losing OTA was a severe blow and we would be further hobbled without the NAS. I would really like to know how we are supposed to get actual quality assessments of the state of scientific understanding if not from convening some of the leaders of the field, getting them to argue it out and write a consensus report, getting the consensus report reviewed, and so forth and so on. The process is messy and imperfect, and occasionally even fails, but these reports have to be done by scientists, and there has to be a careful and uniform protocol set up. And of course, when you do set up the advisory process properly, you are pretty well assured of getting more reliable information than if, say, you just have the president sit down and talk with a sci-fi novelist (to choose a non-random example). And everyone pretty much accepts this... except maybe for Steve Fuller.

Just one more point in reply to him, on the subject of science and democracy. I obviously don't want to suspend the democratic process in favor of some form of technocracy (talk about a straw man). Rather, I want to forge a more productive relationship between scientists and policymakers within the context of democracy, which will inevitably require setting up the scientific advisory process right. But that doesn't mean I should have been out doing man-on-the-street interviews about science policy. This is obviously a fairly rarefied area, one in which political abuses will not even be noticed by much of the public, much less punished at the ballot box. We need a public that better understands science, and we need better science education, but I'm not sure that improving either of these situations will necessarily help us to cope with the extremely sophisticated political attacks on scientific information that we're seeing right now in American government.

And that, I think, provides an adequate reply to the Fuller treatise. Anyway, I needn't defend myself further: John Quiggin has got my back in his second post. What he says. And thanks to you all for contributing.

originally posted March 27th, 2006
http://crookedtimber.org/2006/03/27/man-you-guys-worked-me-hard/

Contributors

JOHN QUIGGIN is a Federation Fellow in economics and political science at the University of Queensland. He is prominent both as an academic economist and as a commentator on public policy.

HENRY FARRELL is assistant professor in the Center for International Science and Technology Policy of the Elliott School of International Affairs, and the Department of Political Science at George Washington University.

TED BARLOW is a litigation consultant. He lives in Houston, TX with his fiancée and their crime-fighting dog.

DANIEL DAVIES began his career at the Bank of England and has been an analyst and stockbroker for ten years. He is a business school graduate, although not strictly a MBA, because there was an MSc in Finance qualification which was substantially cheaper.

JOHN HOLBO is an assistant professor of philosophy at the National University of Singapore.

TIM LAMBERT is a computer scientist at the University of New South Wales.

STEVE FULLER is Professor of Sociology at the University of Warwick, UK. He is associated with the research programme of 'social epistemology', the name of the journal he founded in

1987 and the first of his twelve books, the latest of which are *The Philosophy of Science and Technology Studies* (Routledge, 2006) and *The New Sociological Imagination* (Sage, 2006).

KIERAN HEALY is an assistant professor of sociology at the University of Arizona. His new book is *Last Best Gifts: Altruism and the Market for Human Blood and Organs* (University of Chicago, 2006).

CHRIS MOONEY – in addition to being the author of *The Republican War on Science* – is the Washington correspondent for *Seed* magazine and a senior correspondent for *The American Prospect* magazine.

Printed in the United States
73096LV00002B/4